Siroj Sorajjakool

Child Prostitution in Thailand
Listening to Rahab

Pre-publication
REVIEW

"Sorajjakool describes child prostitution in a comprehensive manner. He is a cultural informant with Western-trained counseling skills, a former international development worker in Thailand, and a theologian. Because of this, he gives dignity to voices we could not otherwise hear. He translates a complex issue that leaves readers enlightened and moved to examine the basis for meaning in their own lives.

This book will be of interest to those in social work, political science, sociology, law, international development, economics, cross-cultural psychology, and theology. Social scientists, development professionals, and economists will benefit from an understanding of how the cycle of poverty started in 1967 with a strategic plan for, ironically, national development. This shifted the focus of national policy from agriculture to industrialization and initiated a cycle of loans in which 'cash became more important than crops.' Thus, cash became the standard for national progress, and with it, for morality and meaning. Sorajjakool skillfully shows how 'the good life' has been socially constructed by consumer and materialistic forces that in turn feed the sex industry even as it depletes the humanity of those who are seduced by it.

The author's training and skill as a counselor are evident. He is not an impartial observer, but seeks meaning by relating it to public policy, indigenous concepts, Buddhism, and theology. 'One becomes a person when one's stories and feelings are acknowledged. . . . Their lives matter when they are heard.' Readers of this book will both hear, and be convinced that these lives matter very much."

Lisa M. Beardsley, PhD, MPH
Vice Chancellor for Academic Affairs and Professor, Department of Health Promotion and Education, Loma Linda University

Child Prostitution in Thailand
Listening to Rahab

Child Prostitution in Thailand
Listening to Rahab

Siroj Sorajjakool

The Haworth Press®
New York • London • Oxford

The Haworth Press, Inc., 10 Alice Street, Binghamton, NY 13904-1580.

TR: 4.15.03

Cover design by Jennifer M. Gaska.

Library of Congress Cataloging-in-Publication Data

Sorajjakool, Siroj.
 Child prostitution in Thailand : listening to Rahab / Siroj Sorajjakool.
  p. cm.
 Includes bibliographical references and index.
 ISBN 0-7890-1494-7 (alk. paper)—ISBN 0-7890-1495-5 (soft)
 1. Child prostitution—Thailand. I. Title.

HQ242.55.A5 S673 2002
306.74'5—dc21

2002068535

To orphans whose parents were victims
of the sex industry in Thailand,
and to those who believe that without dreams,
we are all orphans.

ABOUT THE AUTHOR

Siroj Sorajjakool, PhD, is Associate Professor of Religion (Pastoral Psychology) at Loma Linda University in Loma Linda, California. He earned his PhD in Theology and Personality (Pastoral Care and Counseling) and his MA in Theological Studies at Claremont School of Theology. He also earned an MA in Religion from Andrews University. He was Associate Director of the Adventist Development and Relief Agency in Thailand and has served as pastor in several churches.

CONTENTS

Preface

I remember sitting in a classroom wearing khaki shorts and a white shirt. In bright red thread embroidered on my shirt was 936, my student ID number. Being in seventh grade was tough. I was going through a physical transformation. I knew something about sex, but no details, until my cousin brought home a book on sex. My friends had girlfriends, and I wanted to have a girlfriend too. So many cute girls were in my class, but I did not know how to charm them. Then there was schoolwork. I did so badly that, while my sisters and friends were enjoying themselves in Chiang Mai, I had to take the train to Bangkok for summer school. I failed my Thai language examination, and I barely made it into eighth grade.

Jan wore a navy blue skirt and a white blouse. I do not know her ID number. She was a village girl who probably studied the same poetry I once read, the same history I once learned. From what I gathered, she was an average student, just like me, and engaged in the same activities—drawing on chalkboards, running in the fields, eating ice cream. But she had to do something that I did not—straining her back planting rice in the field. She probably went without meals occasionally. She must have realized that options other than planting rice were available to her, especially when other village girls returned from the south wearing pretty dresses and makeup.

At fourteen, I wondered whether summer school would ever come to an end. At thirteen, Jan wondered whether school would ever come to an end so that she could embark on a new journey, the path toward prosperity. At fourteen, I knew about sex, but Jan, at fourteen, was having sex with clients. Six years after she embarked on this journey that was meant to lead her toward prosperity, her obituary was written.

I remember sitting in the heat of the summer, listening to my teacher, and all I could think was, "Why do I have to sit here and study? I want to get out and play." I wonder what Jan was thinking, lying in bed with clients when she was fourteen? A fourteen-year-old having sex with clients is such a foreign concept—a different world. It is this world that I am trying to comprehend. The following pages are my attempt.

This attempt could not have been realized without a number of individuals who have been most supportive and encouraging. Warren Scale, Associate Director of Adventist Development and Relief Agency Australia, allocated a budget that made my trip to Thailand possible. He also traveled with us for a week, videotaping interviews, offering suggestions, and engaging in discussions on the topic of child prostitution. Busarin Wareesantip, an old friend, drove me around Bangkok, arranged interviews with prostitutes, and was most helpful throughout the interview process. Chrissana Leiw, although she could not travel with us, spent much time making connections that were most fruitful for this project. These three individuals played a central role in my research and I could not have done the job without them. I wish to thank my dean at the Faculty of Religion, Gerald Winslow, for encouraging me and giving me time to engage in this project. My son, Chanchai Sorajjakool, had to assume much more responsibility at home while I was gone for seven weeks, just so I could work on this project. My wife, Hui-Ling, spent her precious spare time editing and offering very helpful suggestions. I am deeply grateful to her for her help and tireless efforts in the midst of her busy schedule. Boonlue and Sumalee Khaisri, grandparents of Got, were most generous in accommodating me at their place, making arrangements for me to interview ex-prostitutes in Chiang Rai, and gathering information on AIDS in Wiang Pa Pao District. I wish to thank Ladawan Wonsriwong, Deputy Minister of Labor and Social Welfare, and her husband, Suwit, for their support. Their tireless efforts in helping these children were a source of inspiration. Another individual who constantly provided encouragement and support is Gayle Foster. Her enthusiasm is a source of courage for me, her sacrifice, a lesson in sharing. My greatest indebtedness belongs to the prostitutes and ex-prostitutes who were willing to share their life stories, their pain, their hopes and dreams.

Introduction

They say my shell is too small
I shrug it off with a smile
For I take pride in my shell
A frog can dream once in a while

Paiwarin Khao-Ngam*
"Under a Coconut Shell"

Sex trade is a multibillion-dollar global industry—an industry of organized crime with complex systems involving influential individuals from gang members to government officials. It is intimidating even to think about the enormity of the problems caused by this industry, and the complication of the systems running it. Hence, this book may be just the dreams of one person, but every inspiration was once only a dream. Some people dream big and turn those dreams into reality. Some children wish their reality was just a dream. They find that choices made in the present bear future consequences: the money they have saved from bearing males' sexual gratification must be spent on medical bills; they have AIDS; their children may not live past the age of three; life is short, and the end will be painful.

A friend said to me, before I left for Thailand, "Go to Thailand and fix the problems of child prostitution." I replied with a smile. I find comfort in the line from Paiwarin Khao-Ngam: "A frog can dream once in a while." Perhaps I may not be able to stop all gang activities. Perhaps I will be unable to cease all sexual violence against children. It may be possible, however, to be there with some of these children as they confront their painful reality. It may be possible to better understand them as people with stories, dreams, sorrow, and courage. It

---

*Excerpts from *Banana Tree Horse* by Paiwarin Khao-Ngam, Bangkok: Amarin Printing and Publishing Public Co., Ltd., Copyright © 1995. Reprinted by permission of the publisher.

may be possible to gather resources so that their dreams may become reality. The following pages reflect my intention to listen to their dreams and to describe their reality. Perhaps, through this whole process of listening, we may discover ourselves through the images of their dreams and the stories of their lives.

I started my journey into the lives of these prostitutes desiring to know and sympathize with victims of such a violent crime. I learned by the end of this journey that we are all victims—not just them. I started my research examining how they felt, only to end it knowing more about how I feel. I questioned their motives, only to learn that mine are questionable as well. I searched for them, only to find us a part of their socialization process—to find that we are victims of our own creation.

METHODOLOGY

I have chosen the subtitle *Listening to Rahab* to reflect the methodology of this book. It is amazing how much we can learn by listening—how much we can learn from prostitutes about life, death, happiness, sadness, family, and isolation. Upon returning from Thailand, I re-read the book of Joshua (Simplified Living Bible) with great interest sparked by numerous conversations with prostitutes, dying ex-prostitutes, agents, politicians, taxi drivers, orphans, men who frequent prostitutes, as well as government/nongovernment officials.

> Then Joshua sent two spies from the camp at Acacia to cross the river. They were to check out the land. They were to take a close look at Jericho. They got to an inn owned by a woman named Rahab. *She was a prostitute.* (Joshua 2:1)

It was through the help of a prostitute that the Israelites were able to spy the promised land. Rahab's family was the only one that survived the attack by the Israelites. Rahab's name was mentioned in the genealogy of Jesus Christ:

> Salmon was the father of Boaz. Rahab was his mother. . . . So there were 14 generations from Abraham to King David. There were 14 from King David's time to the exile. And there were 14 from the exile in Babylon to the time of Christ. (Matthew 1:5, 17)

What was so unique about Rahab that she was able to save her family from the destruction in Jericho and have her name mentioned in the genealogy of Jesus? She was a prostitute who feared God and believed in the God of the Israelites. Her conversation with the spies was recorded in the book of Joshua.

> "I know that your God is going to give my country to you," she told them. "We are all afraid of you. We are filled with fear if the word Israel is even spoken. For we have heard how the Lord dried up the Red Sea for you when you left Egypt! And we know what you did to Sihon and Og, the two Amorite kings east of the Jordan. We heard how you ruined their land and destroyed their people. No wonder we are afraid of you! No one has any fight left after hearing things like that! For your God is the supreme God of heaven. He is not just an ordinary god. Now I beg you for just one thing. Make a promise to me by the holy name of your God. Tell me that when Jericho is conquered you will let me live. Also let my father and mother, my brothers and sisters, and all their families live. This is only fair after the way I have helped you."(Joshua 2:9-13)

I wonder about Rahab. What was she like? Why did she fear God? Why was she willing to risk her life in order to save the spies? How did she feel about her profession? What were her stories? I wonder, if we had the chance to listen to Rahab, what would we learn from her?

There are numerous organizations with plans and strategies for economic development, law enforcement, sponsorships, prevention, and rehabilitation. All these attempts are a step in the right direction, yet one perspective needs to be added: People are people, and their lives matter, when they are heard. Their emptiness takes on meaning when they are no longer simply victims of sex crimes, statistics, or objects of philanthropic generosity. An individual has stories, feelings, and opinions. An individual becomes a person when those stories, feelings, and opinions are acknowledged.

SOURCES OF INFORMATION
AND THE COLLECTION OF STORIES

On January 2, 2001, I left for Thailand to pursue a research project dealing with the problems of child prostitution by looking at cases in

Thailand. I wanted their stories to speak for them. I interviewed ten prostitutes and ex-prostitutes. One passed away at the age of nineteen. Four have tested HIV positive. One planned to return to a brothel in the south. Two were approximately sixteen years old. Five entered the sex industry at the age of fourteen or fifteen, and the rest, at the age of eighteen or older. Of the nine who are still alive, four do not have much time left. One of the ten was from northeast Thailand. The rest were from Chiang Rai Province near the Thai-Burmese border in northern Thailand.

Besides these girls, I interviewed government officials running a rehabilitation center in Pa-kred, a member of the Thai Parliament who currently serves as deputy minister of the Ministry of Labor and Social Welfare, a current and an ex-sex trade agent, taxi drivers, men who frequent prostitutes,[1] staff members at the Centre for the Protection of Children's Rights (CPCR) and at End Child Prostitution in Asian Tourism (ECPAT), the project director for Thai Women of Tomorrow, villagers in Chiang Rai, and poor families in Phayao Province.

PURPOSE

My deepest desire in writing these pages is to dust off the mirror in the corner of our consciousness so that we may recognize their stories as our stories; their poverty, our thirst; their survival, our gratification. I wish for us to see ourselves through their tears and realize that we are all victims of the human socialization process. These girls were products of their society, just as we are governed by our own social norms. "What will give them the courage to decide differently?" is the question that we need to ask ourselves. What will give us the courage to act on what we believe to be good and true in the face of social pressure and contrary societal norms? Perhaps with such courage we can turn dreams into reality. I submit, too, that perhaps spirituality is that very source of courage, the force that actualizes dreams.

ORGANIZATION

Most chapters begin with stories. I have chosen to follow the life story of one woman, Tabtim, whose child became a victim of trafficking when an Indonesian trafficker used him as a decoy to bring a Chinese girl to Los Angeles. Local nongovernmental organizations (NGOs) and some Thai newspapers in Los Angeles described her as irresponsible. Her relatives believe that she was lured into the sex industry in Chiang Mai at the age of twelve; she sees her career differently. Portions of her story appear in various chapters, and the context of her story forms the platform for the description of various aspects of child prostitution problems in Thailand.

Chapter 1 describes the story of my encounter with a Hmong girl by the name of Ju whose mother threatened to sell her. It discusses the peak period of child prostitution in Thailand and the factors contributing to its growth. Chapter 2 discusses the changing forms of child prostitution by examining three factors that contribute to these changes, including the impact of the Prevention and Suppression of Prostitution Act (1996) on the proliferation of entertainment businesses.

The portrayal of the early life of Tabtim, a girl who entered the sex industry at the age of fifteen, helps to introduce the issue of poverty, which is the main focus of Chapter 3. This chapter discusses the level of poverty and its impact on prostitution and the problem of children entering this business. Chapter 4 focuses on how these girls entered the sex trade and the different forms of the sex industry. The issue of parenting is briefly discussed. In Tabtim's case, her mother played an important role in her decision to leave to work in a restaurant in Chiang Mai.

Chapter 5 looks at men who frequent prostitutes and reflects on cultural values and norms that perpetuate the problem of prostitution. Chapter 6 considers reasons these young women return home and examines the issue of AIDS in Thailand's northern provinces.

Chapter 7 starts with the story of a little boy who was the victim of trafficking. It explores the problem of trafficking in both Thailand and the United States, various forms of trafficking and the structures of these organizations, and the problems that confront NGOs and government agencies struggling with the issue of trafficking.

The last chapter closes with my reflections on the problems of prostitution: What does this issue say about us and our socialization process? What can we learn from these girls who at one time or another permitted their bodies to be used to gratify males' lust?

Chapter 1

Ju and Other Stories: Selling Children

The rice bird had dwelt on the grassy knoll,
Cherishing its dreams, clouds, freedom and soul;
One day, a raging storm tore its world apart;
Its fate thus altered, so sadly it must depart.

Homeless in the urban heap,
In which hold do you sleep?
What snare entraps you;
And the trapper is who?

Paiwarin Khao-Ngam
"Rice Bird"

Children are supposed to play catch, eat ice cream, and laugh with their friends. I recall with delight those afternoons my grandfather took me to eat coconut ice cream and played boxing with me. Of course, I have heard sad stories of children whose dreams of laughter never become reality, but this has always been only a cognitive realization, a mental picture.

I was born a dreamer with a great fondness for ideas. Somehow I became more fascinated with these ideas than with actuality. Chasing ideas was a natural part of me. At a certain point in life, though, one becomes disillusioned with ideas and seeks actuality. For me, this happened when I was teaching in a seminary. Theology, I thought, must now be incarnated. It was a rather simplistic idea, but I had to start somewhere.

SELLING CHILDREN

In June 1992, I loaded fifteen theology students into a pickup truck and drove north along winding roads up the mountainside to a Hmong village in Petchaboon Province. Our goal was to build fifty toilets in ten days. We lived in a run-down *anubarn,* or kindergarten, with cracks in the wooden walls. A pair of eyes continually peeked through those cracks the entire time we were there. Those eyes belonged to Ju. She was eleven at the time and always carried her nephew on her back. Unlike all her friends in the village, she did not go to school. Her parents were very poor and her father was an opium addict. Her only option was to baby-sit her aunt's son in exchange for food and lodging.

The night before we left the village Ju came to see Phayom, one of my students whom she had gotten to know fairly well.

"I need to talk to you," she whispered.

"Of course."

"Not here. I need to talk to you in private."

They both walked to a little room at the school. Ju asked, "Your group seems to be laughing and smiling all the time. Tell me, why are all of you so happy all the time?"

Phayom told her about God and Christianity and hope and happiness. She noticed that Ju just stared at the floor with an obvious expression of sadness. "What's wrong?" Phayom asked. There was a long pause and tears before a reply.

"I want to die," responded Ju.

"Why?"

"Because I hate my mom. Because she wants to sell me off."[1]

I had heard about children whose sadness is far greater than their laughter, whose tears outnumber their smiles. Now I see. I thought children were supposed to smile and play, but Ju's story is a reality I cannot deny. This encounter was the beginning of my interest in the subject of child prostitution. Reading about this issue led to shocking discoveries:

> A 16-year-old Cambodian girl woke up to find herself in a small brothel in her country's capital, Phnom Penh. Her aunt had drugged her into unconsciousness and handed her over to a brothel owner in exchange for money.[2]

According to the report, when she refused to sleep with the customers, the brothel owner drugged her with a different type of substance that left her awake, but submissive. They took her to a hotel room where she was forced to have sex with several men. After spending a week in this brothel, she was sent to Battambang, Cambodia's second-largest city. At this brothel, she was locked in a room and was once whipped with an electric cord. She regained her freedom when the police raided this brothel in August 1995.

The story of Nuan, a fourteen-year-old girl from Roi Et Province in Thailand, is rather common. Nuan has an older sister. Her parents are farmers whose bodies have borne the raging heat of the sun while planting rice in the field. Nuan recalled with fondness days when she used to play in the rice field: "We were poor but villagers were friendly and kind. They always extended hospitality to one another." Soon, through commercials and mass media, things began to change. Technology was introduced into the village in the name of progress and development. Villagers started competing with one another and comparing commodities. Women even compared dresses. To Nuan, this so-called development blinded their souls and perpetuated greed, especially in the case of her father. "He did not know how to be a dad anymore," she recalled.

When Nuan's older sister became a teenager, their father sent her to work in Bangkok. Nuan and her mother never knew the type of work that her sister did. One night when she was in grade five, Nuan's innocence was stolen from her by her own father, when he came into her room late in the night and touched her body like a man whose morality is blinded by passion. This continued for one year. For Nuan, it was a torturous year of conflicted feelings and confusion, sorrow and betrayal. She had managed to complete grade six when her sister returned from Bangkok. Hope grew in Nuan's heart when her father announced that she would be sent to study in Bangkok. It was an escape door from sex and betrayal for her. Little did she know of her father's plan.

When she arrived in Bangkok, her sister took her to a go-go bar in Patpong[3] where her sister once worked. She watched her sister negotiate with a couple, and then that couple took Nuan to the back room. A foreigner entered and gave her a quick lesson in English, not the type of education she was hoping to get in Bangkok. After the lesson, Nuan received instructions on how to dance and solicit clients. To have her hope taken away was perhaps more painful for Nuan than having no hope at all.

Nuan's sister gave her a white pill each night before she started dancing in the go-go bar. It was a consciousness-altering chemical that left Nuan lost on a stage amid flashing lights, pounding music, and shiny metallic poles. Moving with the rhythm, entertaining clients through seductive gestures while undressing, this fourteen-year-old girl who just wanted to go to school soon found herself lying in bed with foreign men, wondering about her father and her sister. For one year she was haunted by the betrayal of her father and sister, the two family members who gained from her pain, the two family members who could quantify commodities and compete with neighbors through the proceeds from her body. Sex was tolerable, but betrayal was more than this little girl could bear. She had a nervous breakdown, was hospitalized, and asked to quit her job. As she started to heal, her father came to persuade her to return to the go-go bar because "[t]he income was much better."[4]

STATISTICS, FACTS, AND FIGURES

Nuan's story is not uncommon. About 450,000 Thai men visit prostitutes every day. The number of prostitutes estimated by CPCR was approximately 2 million. Of this figure, 800,000 were below the age of eighteen and 200,000 were twelve or younger.[5] Discussion on the number of child prostitutes in Thailand has been engaged in by various organizations and professionals who researched the field. The number of prostitutes suggested by various researchers ranges from 65,000 to 2.8 million.[6] According to the 1990 population census, in Thailand, 8.3 million women are in the fifteen to twenty-nine age range, the most common ages for prostitutes.[7] Further, most prostitutes work in urban areas. Thus, 2.8 million would equate with 24 to 34 percent of women in this age range, or every woman in this age range who lives in an urban area. This number seems unrealistically high. Research by Jenny Godley in 1991 produced an estimate of 700,000 female sex workers.[8] This number works out to about 8.5 percent of women in this age range, or 24 percent of urban women. This figure seems a little high, but possible. Based on their ethnographic studies in 1991, Sittirai Veerasit and Tim Brown reached an estimate of

150,000 to 200,000 prostitutes, or 1.8 to 2.4 percent of the women in this age range and 6.3 to 8.3 percent of urban women.[9] How does this estimate reflect the numbers in child prostitution? Reports show that 17 percent of prostitutes visiting health clinics for checkups were below the age of eighteen. Based on Veerasit and Brown's calculations, the number of child prostitutes, according to Phongpaichit and colleagues, ranges from approximately 25,500 to 34,000.[10]

Stories of child prostitution are terrifying. For example:

> These girls, when sold, are usually locked up in the brothels, often not seeing the light of day for up to two years. They can be called on for sex 24 hours a day. The usual working hours of these girls start from 10 a.m. to 4 a.m. The price of a virgin girl is between 2,000-15,000 baht. This amount goes to the brothels. Each visit after is between 100-150 baht. If the customer desires to stay overnight, he is charged 200 baht. The highest return for these girls is 50% of the price charged while the lowest is approximately 5%. Wages are not usually paid in cash to the girls but recorded in their accounts. They are given $1.20 each day for meals. Each girl is forced to accept a minimum of 1-2 customers per day and a maximum of 26 customers per day.[11]

According to Aurasom Suthisakorn, some good-looking girls were forced to entertain from twenty to twenty-six customers per night from 7:00 p.m. to 1:00 a.m., which is approximately one client every fifteen minutes.[12]

I have heard that of the 1,000 children rescued from fifty brothels by various social welfare organizations, 20 percent were HIV positive. CPCR reported that, on June 4, 1991, seventeen young tribal girls between eleven and seventeen years of age were rescued from a brothel in Phuket. One of the girls was forced to entertain customers even when she was seven months pregnant. In April 1991, a teahouse was raided and 100 girls were rescued, of which ten were below the age of sixteen. Twenty of these girls were tricked or coerced into prostitution. Seventeen out of these twenty girls were HIV positive. In November of the same year, a brothel in Rayong Province was raided and twelve girls were rescued: "Most of the girls had been physically abused with plastic pipes and raped before being forced into prostitution. Blood tests indicated that 11 out of 12 were HIV positive."[13]

In her book *Sanim Dokmai*, Aurasom Suthisakorn described a pimp taming a girl who refused to cooperate. The pimp took the sharp, curved edge of an iron hanger to whip the bare back of the girl then dragged it down to the waist, pulling the skin off her back.[14]

FEELINGS

When we listen to such stories we wonder about the souls and psyches of these children, the mental and emotional pain they experience. Most of the children in this category meet the diagnostic criteria of post-traumatic stress disorder. They experience recurring images of trauma such as rape, beating, and screaming. They are highly agitated and irritable and suffer from heightened anxiety. They obsessively think, question, and search for reasons their parents sold them and pimps beat them. "What's wrong with me?" is a question often asked. These thoughts continually cycle, and the children sink deeper into depression, until it causes an incredible darkness in their souls. Their depression reinforces a sense of emptiness and worthlessness, and passing thoughts of suicide appear more and more to be an attractive option.[15]

Most of us in the United States have the privilege of seeing therapists when we experience depression. Even then, coping with such pain brings misery. However, for these children who sink deep into depression, instead of seeing therapists, they have to smile, freshen up, entertain clients, and bear that sense of filth within their souls. The only words to provide solace are those of the invisible author from the imagination of Kahlil Gibran comforting Marta al-Baniyah:

> The body's filth cannot touch the pure soul, and snowdrifts cannot destroy living seeds. This life is but a threshing floor of sorrows in which souls have their adversities sifted out before they give their yield. . . . You are oppressed, Marta, and the one who wronged you is the owner of mansions, the possessor of great wealth and a small soul.[16]

In the words of one thirteen-year-old girl, Sawai Chandee, "At night, I sleep and cry. No one ever sees my tears."[17]

SAVING CHILDREN

Stories of unspeakable cruelty against children force one to confront their plight. I am not truly fond of children. I do not know how to play with nor entertain them. I avoid them whenever possible, but when you can feel the emptiness of their souls as you look into their eyes, avoidance is no longer an option. My soul became restless, and I asked, "What could possibly be done for these children?"

In July 1999, during another toilet-building trip to Thailand, I made an appointment to meet Ladawan Wongsriwong, who at that time served as deputy secretary to the prime minister of Thailand and president of the Young Northern Women's Development Foundation. I had heard stories of her struggles to help children escape prostitution and wanted to know what I could do to help.

Ms. Wongsriwong's project seeks to prevent children who complete grade six from entering prostitution through awarding scholarships for them to continue in school. Her rationale for emphasizing education is based on a number of surveys which show that 30 percent of young girls who complete a sixth grade education do not go on to grade seven for financial reasons. Of this population, 90 percent will end up in different brothels. Offering opportunities for these children to continue their education helps prevent them from entering the sex trade. Hence, according to Ms. Wongsriwong, an educational program that targets the most vulnerable population can be an important tool in the prevention of child prostitution. This at-risk population refers to children from very poor families (income bracket of 10,000 baht or less per year), with a family history of prostitution, and children who lack the opportunity and funds to continue their education. The foundation works with schoolteachers in this area who understand the living and financial situations of these children.

After learning of the benefits this project offers to at-risk children, through the help of the Thai Seventh-Day Adventist Church, I invited Ms. Wongsriwong to Southern California to speak to a number of academic institutions and Thai communities. We were able to raise some scholarship funds and were proud to take part in the prevention of child prostitution.

Curiosity

Being trained in pastoral counseling, I often wonder about the intrapsychic process of children sold and traumatized by their experiences. How do they cope with the pain that has never been resolved? My readings in this area offer me the impression that most of these girls deal with depression through isolation or substance abuse. Sexual promiscuity is also not uncommon. Returning to prostitution, therefore, may seem a viable option, especially since they must earn enough to maintain their drug habits. I was unable to find more specific information on the intrapsychic process of this population of children being coerced into prostitution. This led to my plan to visit Thailand to gather firsthand information through interviews. When I arrived in Thailand, not only did I not have access to this population due to institutional restrictions, I found very different stories from what I had anticipated.

Chapter 2

From Coercion to Personal Decision: Changing Forms of Child Prostitution

Born elsewhere, whence come, they are
All aiming for fame and fortune,
In the capital, gathering from afar,
Seek their welfare opportune.

Paiwarin Khao-Ngam
"Bangkok Mood"

Anticipating hearing stories of children being coerced into prostitution prior to my trip to Thailand, I arranged with a retired public health worker in Pa-Ngiew, Chiang Rai, to interview three girls sold into prostitution before the age of eighteen. He told me that it would be easy to locate this entry-level group. Upon my arrival, I interviewed only one girl, and she did not enter prostitution until the age of twenty-seven. My next stop was ECPAT International, an office located in downtown Bangkok. During my conversation with Chitraporn Vanaspongse, Information Officer, I learned that the number of children coerced into prostitution has dropped, and that fewer children at the ages of fourteen and fifteen enter this trade. The economic crisis and the Prevention and Suppression of Prostitution Act of 1996 led to the emergence of a new group of sex workers: high school and college students between the ages of eighteen and twenty-two. During this conversation, I still believed that a large number of children are coerced and lured into prostitution. I kept asking questions about this population but did not get the answers I expected.

My trip to Kred Trakarn Welfare Protection and Vocational Development Center confirmed Vanaspongse's description of the changing demographics of child prostitution. A social worker at this rehabilitation center informed me that the rehabilitation center runs a vocational program for approximately 200 girls. Of this number, only twenty-five below the age of eighteen are employed in some form of the sex industry. Of these twenty-five girls, only five had been coerced into prostitution (see Tables 2.1, 2.2, and 2.3).

Table 2.3 provides a clear picture of the general distribution of the girls in the sex industry. In the past, most girls entering this business usually came from the north. These northern girls represented the population of girls who were lured, coerced, and sold by their parents. It was uncommon to hear of northeastern and central girls entering this trade back then. Now the picture is changing, with most girls being from the latter areas. Further, only five of the twenty-five girls (20 percent) were coerced into prostitution and traumatized by the events.

Many conversations with various individuals on this same topic convinced me that the sex industry in Thailand is indeed changing. A taxi driver who took my friends and me through the red-light districts in Chiang Mai said, "You can hardly find young girls being sold into prostitution anymore. Most of them volunteer their services."

"Are girls still being forced or sold into prostitution?" I asked.

"Probably, but they are the minority. These are probably girls who borrowed money from pimps, and so they have to be kept within strict boundaries until they repay the loan," he replied.

TABLE 2.1. Children in the Kred Trakarn Rehabilitation Center by Age

Age (years)	15	16	17	18
Number of Girls	2	13	8	2

TABLE 2.2. Children in the Kred Trakarn Rehabilitation Center by Education

Grade	No education	2	4	5	6	7	8	9	AA
Number	1	1	2	5	7	1	2	5	1

TABLE 2.3. Children in the Kred Trakarn Rehabilitation Center by Area

Area	Northeast	Central	West	North
Number	8	11	3	3

My final confirmation on this issue came a couple of days before I left Thailand. I had a conversation with Pantip Watanapornpongsook, a CPCR staff member, and she later faxed me their reports on the number of child prostitutes; starting in 1988, the number peaked in 1990 and dropped sharply between 1992 and 1993 (the report is based on the number of children rescued by CPCR) (see Figure 2.1). The report also indicates that, in 1998, only fifteen children were rescued from the sex industry by CPCR.[1] These figures and information raised more questions: Is it true that there are fewer child prostitutes in Thailand? Does "fewer children rescued from the sex industry," as reported by both the Kred Trakarn rehabilitation center and CPCR mean that fewer children are in prostitution?

While conversing with Chakrapan Wongburanavart, director of Thai Women of Tomorrow, I asked, "Is it true that there are fewer children in prostitution?"

"It is true that there may be fewer children in prostitution but the number is not significant," was the reply.

"What about all the stories I have heard regarding the success of educational programs for the prevention of child prostitution?"

Yr.	80	81	82	83	84	85	86	87	88	89	90	91	92	93	94	95	96
No.	0	0	2	2	3	9	16	28	179	78	377	237	218	49	29	23	16

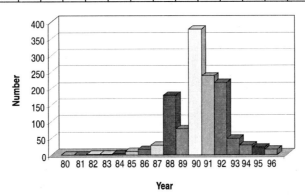

FIGURE 2.1. Number of Child Prostitutes Rescued by the Centre for the Protection of Children's Rights

"The programs supported and operated by various NGOs have been very successful. There has been a dramatic reduction in the number of child prostitutes in areas where these NGOs have been working."

"So why are there still many children in prostitution if the programs have been successful?" I probed.

"There has been a significant reduction in the number of provinces that we have been working with. The problem is, there is an emerging group from a different population. These are girls from high schools and colleges volunteering their services to support their lifestyle, their families, or themselves through school."

It is also interesting to note that between 1980 and the early 1990s, 90 percent of Thai prostitutes in Japan were tricked into the sex trade. However, between 1995 and 1996, this population dropped to 20 percent (see Figure 2.2). "In other words, about 80 percent of the women going to Japan in the mid-1990s had the explicit intention of working in sex services."[2]

Yet another population fills the gap left by children in northern provinces who are now continuing with their education: illegal immigrants. These are tribal girls from the north and girls from Burma and China.

A fourteen-year-old girl from Mae Sai wrote:

> In Mae Sai there are many occupations. There are both many people and many occupations for them. But the occupation that most people know in Mae Sai is prostitution, because it is well known in Mae Sai. This occupation has girls from Myanmar, Laos and from other places. The girls in this profession come into it on their own free will because their own countries are not that developed and thus they come here. The girls have not studied thus this is their main profession to gain money. Some of them have come into Thailand legally, while others have entered illegally by boat, across the Mae Sai River that forms the border. Some girls will be sent by their parents to sell their bodies, their parents do not have money and thus they have to send their children to Thailand.[3]

FACTORS CONTRIBUTING TO THIS CHANGE

At least three factors led to this change. The first factor is the 1996 Prevention and Suppression of Prostitution Act, which inflicts severe

Child Prostitution 1980-1995

Girls who volunteered

10%

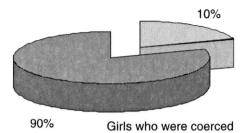

90%   Girls who were coerced

Child Prostitution 1995-Present

Girls who were coerced

20%

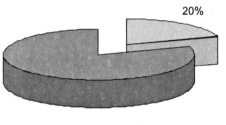

80%   Girls who volunteered

FIGURE 2.2. Comparison of Children Who Voluntarily Entered and Children Coerced into Prostitution

punishment on those engaged in the sex industry that involves children and parents who sell their children. This act created a significant reduction in the number of brothels in Thailand, but also plays an important role in the growth of sex industry not involving negotiating sex with children. This is in no way suggesting that the law is not well written or conceived. It definitely plays a very significant role in the prevention of child prostitution.

The Suppression of Prostitution Act, B.E. 2503 (1960) was intended to wipe out all forms of prostitution in Thailand, which was legalized prior to 1960. This act punished prostitutes more severely than procurers. An arrested prostitute could face imprisonment for three to six months and a fine of 1,000 to 2,000 baht, according to the act of prostitution. Prostitutes could be retained for rehabilitation for up to two years. Procurers, on the other hand, faced up to three months of imprisonment and a 1,000-baht fine with no rehabilitation. In assessing the 1960 suppression act, Wanchai Roujanavong, Senior Expert State Attorney, Office of the Attorney General, stated:

> When prostitutes themselves were targets of suppression and were treated as criminals, they were pushed into protection of procurers who had influence with law enforcement officials. Not only did the Act fail to suppress prostitution as planned, but the Act also encouraged prostitution to be widespread and increased in numbers and forms. Within the period of 36 years the Act had been in use, prostitution had grown and prospered unchecked. Organized criminal rings benefited from prostitution business grew stronger with increasing influence and power.[4]

The present act, which came into effect December 21, 1996, sees prostitutes as victims of poverty and organized crime. Hence, its primary aim is to punish procurers, brothel owners, mama-sans, pimps, customers, and parents who sell their children. Punishment of procurers is stated in Section 9:

> Any person who procures, seduces or takes away any person for the prostitution of such person, even with her or his consent and irrespective of whether the various acts which constitute an offence are committed within or outside the Kingdom, shall be liable to imprisonment for a term of one to ten years and to a fine of twenty thousand to two hundred thousand Baht.
>
> If the offence under paragraph one is committed against a person over fifteen but not over eighteen years of age, the offender shall be liable to imprisonment for a term of five to fifteen years and to a fine of one hundred thousand to three hundred thousand Baht.
>
> If the offence under paragraph one is committed against a child not over fifteen years of age, the offender shall be liable to imprisonment for a term of ten to twenty years and to a fine of two hundred thousand to four hundred thousand Baht.[5]

Terms of punishment for parents selling their own children for sexual service is stated in Section 10:

> Any person who, being a father, mother or parent of a person not over eighteen years of age, knows of the commission against the person under his or her parental control of the offence under paragraph two, paragraph three or paragraph four of section 9 and connives at such commission shall be liable to imprisonment for a term of four to twenty years and to a fine of eighty thousand to four hundred thousand Baht.[6]

In Section 11, the same terms are applied to the owner, supervisor, or manager of a prostitution business or establishment. The younger the prostitutes, the heavier the punishment. The punishment becomes more serious when crime against prostitutes turns violent. Section 12 states:

> Any person who detains or confines another person, or by any other means, deprives such person of the liberty of person or causes bodily harm to or threatens in any manner whatsoever to commit violence against another person in order to compel such other person to engage in prostitution shall be liable to imprisonment for a term of ten to twenty years and to a fine of two hundred thousand to four hundred thousand Baht.

> If the commission of the offence under paragraph one results in:

> (1) grievous bodily harm being caused to the victim, the offender shall be liable to imprisonment for life;
> (2) death being caused to the victim, the offender shall be liable to death penalty or to imprisonment for life.[7]

The mushrooming of various types of sex industry, such as restaurants and cafés, karaoke, cocktail lounges, and *salaya dong,*[8] is, according to many staff workers of various NGOs, partially the result of the Prevention and Suppression of Prostitution Act of 1996. Chitraporn Vanaspongse of ECPAT International, who used to observe young girls walking around in Pattaya soliciting clients, said, "After 1996 you can't find these girls by the street soliciting clients. They are now working in bars or karaokes." It is still about sex, but the form has changed. Owners of these various types of sex business are also circumventing the law, becoming quite creative in supplying sex for cash without getting caught. For example, a restaurant owner will hire a girl to work until midnight or one in the morning. The girl's salary depends on this working hour. However, if a client wishes to sleep with a girl, that client will have to pay the owner 1,500 baht to "off" (slang for taking a girl out for sex) her to a motel or hotel. In this way, both the owner and the girl are paid for providing sexual service to the client. Although the girl may be paid for sex, the owner is also compensated for the girl's working hour. It does not matter if the girl leaves the restaurant at 11:00 p.m. or earlier; the same payment is due to the owner. It is understood that none of these girls is paid 1,500 baht for two or more hours. The law cannot fault the owner for providing sexual services, however, because the owner does not get paid for providing sex; the owner is compensated for the worker's lost time. As far as the owner is concerned, the sexual negotiation is between the girl and the client.

The second factor driving the change in the sex industry involves the education campaigns by various governmental agencies and NGOs, which have significantly reduced the number of girls from northern provinces entering into prostitution. These programs focus on instilling a sense of pride and dignity among young girls, teaching them that prostitution is not the solution, and offering them alternatives through career training or educational scholarships. These campaigns best explain the phrase I commonly heard while visiting northern Thailand: "Children in our area no longer work as prostitutes."

The final factor behind the change is consumerism, which has fostered a generation of young girls who opt for the life of prostitution to maintain a "better" lifestyle. When products that flood markets dictate lifestyle, society redefines how one ought to live, living by the rules designed by advertising agencies. City girls need to supplement their income so that they can go to school, pay rent, fit in, support their families, and carry mobile phones. According to the research "Factors That Lead Young Girls to Enter Prostitution in Chiang Mai," by Thai Women of Tomorrow, Chiang Mai University, every single girl in their sample population who volunteered her sex services did so because of her level of poverty. If given an alternative, none of them would have chosen prostitution.[9]

Chapter 3

Ban Pongnong: Living in Poverty

How many fields and acres are worked,
Torments and ordeals shirked,
Lives, eras and eons lived,
Strifes and struggles survived,
Ploughs and sickles produced,
Oxen and buffaloes used,
Serfdom's sufferings endured,
Before our freedom's procured?

How much ache and pain do we bear
Rain, fire, losing, winning must we dare?

Paiwarin Khao-Ngam
"The Heartland"

In our civil minds, it is inconceivable how parents could sell their children. The existence of children selling their bodies voluntarily, however, disturbs us even more deeply and questions the very core of our humanity. What can lead a child even to consider this an alternative?

The following report appeared in May 4, 2000: "Tabtim Kaew-taengian, a 22-year-old former masseuse who has remarried and is now a housewife, denies an allegation by her mother that she may have sold him to a human smuggling group."[1] In an interview with Thai Independent Television, Tabtim claimed that she had allowed her son to go sight-seeing with an Indonesian man, similar to previous occasions. She was not aware that the man was taking her son to the United States. She first learned that her son was in the United States when she received a call from U.S. immigration.

GOT

One evening in May 2000 I received a call from Ladawan Wongs-riwong, President of the Young Northern Women's Development Foundation.

"Have you heard the case of the little Thai boy by the name of 'Got'?" she asked.

"No, I have not," I replied.

"This is a big case in Thailand with lots of news coverage. The little boy entered the United States using a fake passport sometime last month—used as a decoy. An Indonesian man was trying to traffic in a Chinese woman to work as a sex worker. They needed him in order to appear as a family in front of the immigration officer. Can you please go and visit the boy to see how he is doing?"

"I'd be glad to," I assured her.

I went to visit Got at the residence of a staff member of the one of the local NGOs. He was fair with distinctive northern Thai features, three years old, and small for his age. He had a slight fever and was trying hard to communicate with this staff member. But because his maternal grandparents in Chiang Rai raised him, his northern Thai dialect and underdeveloped language skills made it difficult for his caretakers to understand. Occasionally he would cry out in frustration over his inability to communicate. He went outside to the backyard to ride his tricycle. I watched him for a while, wondering about his life, and his mother.

Tabtim

> His mother, Tabtim Kaewtaengjan, was sold into sexual slavery at age 12, according to Thai press reports. Both sides believe she is a drug addict and unfit to raise a child, particularly since she is now married to a man suspected of running a trafficking ring.[2]

While an NGO, the INS and the Thai government were negotiating the case of Got, I left for Thailand to research issues regarding children and the sex industry there. A couple of days before I left Thailand to return to California, I managed to secure Tabtim's phone number. I called around 9:00 p.m., and a man picked up the phone. He was rather suspicious of me and asked who gave me Tabtim's phone number. I told him that I got it from her mother-in-law. He hesitated and then called Tabtim to the phone. It was the first time I had talked with her. Her voice was gentle as she spoke with her northern Thai accent. She seemed ready to trust me. I asked if we could meet so that I could hear her story. She did not hesitate and suggested a place where we could meet.

On February 15, around 10:00 a.m., we met at Robinson Mall, located on Ratchadapisak Road in Bangkok. Tabtim is fair, as are most northern Thai women, and there is also something very Chinese about her look. As we sat at the eating area, I told her that I had visited her son in Los Angeles a couple of times. She asked how he was doing. I told her that he was doing well and putting on weight. I noticed a smile on her face. As I sat across from her reflecting on the stories I heard, numerous questions came to mind. What was it like to read negative descriptions of oneself printed across the headlines of various newspapers? What was it like to be called a prostitute, an unfit mother, a drug addict, a mother who sells her own flesh and blood? I posed these questions and the immediate response was silence. She was disturbed by them. She had read all the descriptions by which the public had characterized her. What saddened her most was being described as a mother who sold her son. "I did not sell my son," she said firmly.

I asked her if she could recount the narrative of her life since she was little until the present. Without any hesitation, she started sharing.

Tabtim is also known as Goung, her nickname which literally translated as "prawn." Her father, Mr. Pratan Kaewpaengchan, still works seasonal odd jobs. Her mother, Tong, is a housewife. Tabtim grew up in Ban Pongnong with her two older brothers. She described her older brother, Karn, as being quiet and rigid. He was a hardworking "loner" with whom she never really got along. He was bossy and liked to order her around the house. When things were not done the way he wanted, he would hit her. On the contrary, Kob, her second brother, was playful and caring.

Tabtim grew up in a wooden house that rested on stilts. The walls of the house were approximately six feet high, with a flat roof made of zinc above the dirt floor. The wood panels were painted dark brown. Underneath the house was an open area where family and friends could gather, with wooden stairs leading up to the front door. The house included a small kitchen on one side, a bedroom, and an open area for sleeping, with not much else, except a cabinet for storing clothes, mattresses, and mosquito nets.

POVERTY

"Behind every face there is a story" is a phrase I often use in teaching my students. When you listen to people's stories, they are no longer the objects of your scrutiny. When you listen, they become individuals. They are no longer just an illness, diagnosis, pathology, and treatment plan.

The story behind the case of Got, which appeared on the front pages of various newspapers, is the story of a girl born and raised in the small village of Ban Pongnong, in Chiang Rai Province. It is also the birthplace of many girls who suffered the same fate as Tabtim. What was it like to be raised in this small village, to live in this house on stilts that barely has anything in it, to be awakened by the sound of the roosters in the morning, to watch your father waiting for a job, and to wonder, "Do we have enough food to last, money to spare, if Dad does not get a call to go work in the field today?"

In recollecting memories of life in the field, Paiwarin Khao-Ngam writes:

> They toil and tell their tales on paper fields,
> Till the land, rake the soil, on empty sheets.
> Dust till dawn, eon of dreams boldly yields
> Rice sown, to await a harvest of love seeds.
>
> Everybody be happy and nice.
> In the water's fish, in the fields rice![3]

"In the water's fish, in the fields rice!" is the story of the past. The present finds sweetness only in remembrance of bygone days. In his poem "Boy, Buffalo, and World," Khao-Ngam captures the mood:

> Remembrances of the past, memories of yore,
> Shuffled to the front and shoved again to the fore,
> Want to lure us back to the lovely time before;
> But, alas, they are too far gone for us to restore.[4]

"No fish in the pond with rice enough to last a couple of meals" is most likely the actual story of present-day farmers. The life of these farmers seems to suggest that poverty indeed begets poverty. The description of such a cycle is well captured in the words of Dominique Lapierre as he sought to depict the life of Prodip Pal in his book *The City of Joy:*

> Just as ten or twelve million other Bengali peasants during this second half of the twentieth century, they were to become the victims of that endemic phenomenon known to economists as the cycle of poverty—that unavoidable process of descending along the social ladder by which the farmer became a sharecropper, then a peasant without land, then an agricultural laborer, then, eventually forced into exile. It was no use even dreaming of climbing a step in the opposite direction. Here everyone had to fight merely to defend his existing status, which was under constant threat. Improvement of that status was quite inconceivable, for poverty can only engender greater poverty. If it is true that coal does not change its color when washed, it is equally true that poverty painted in even the most dazzling colors remains forever poverty.[5]

Farmers

The cycle of poverty for farmers in Thailand probably started in 1957 with the initiation of a strategic plan for national development. It was a change in national policy, a movement from agriculture toward industrialization.[6] The policy aimed at bridging the gap between the rich and the poor. Or was it "poverty painted in even the most dazzling colors"?

According to Kanoksak Kaewthep, an economist, the two factors that greatly affect the economic status of farmers and perpetuate the cycle of poverty are land ownership and industrialization. A couple of years ago, I had the opportunity to visit a Hmong village in Phayao Province. I was told that these villagers used to stay in the forest reserve area. Then the government relocated them to Ban Sob Kam, promising five acres of land per family. After they did not see the "promised land" for a couple of years, they pursued this promise for a number of years, until they saw the land allocated for them. They bent down to touch the soil, only to feel rocks in their hands. The land was not suitable for agriculture. To survive, the villagers spend two to three months in the forests picking fruits to sell in the market. Their annual income averages 5,000 baht (US$125).[7]

Stories of farmers in Ban Buak is a reminder of the price some had to pay for land. Due to the limitations of farmland, the villagers expanded their territory to increase production by using parts of forest land in Pa Ban Pang Muang. At the same time, rich investors, through collaboration with some government officials, started cutting down trees in areas where farmers were planting rice and vegetables. Villagers, together with a group of student activists in the north, marched to the city hall in Lampang Province and, in front of the parliament, demanded justice. The ownership of the land was granted to these farmers, but at a very costly price: many leaders in this protest were murdered.[8]

The other factor, according to Kaewthep, is the movement toward industrialization. Table 3.1 clearly shows why the expression "In the water fish, in the field rice!" is a memory of the past.[9]

The Farmers Union was organized in 1974 to protest the development plan that failed to recognize the importance of farmers. The government decided to incorporate strategies that would enhance the production of agriculture, but the attempt only led to a widening of the gap. Economic growth intoxicates, and the nation gave in to the seductive power of cash, technology, and conveniences. Thus, the cycle of poverty continues.[10]

Thirty some years ago, farmers owned thirty rai (2.5 rai per acre) of land per family. Thirty years later, they own ten rai per family,

TABLE 3.1. Comparison of Agricultural and Industrial Products in Thailand

Year	Agriculture (%)	Industry (%)
1965	34.8	22.7
1980	25.4	28.5
1985	19.5	29.2
1988	16.9	32.5
1992	12.0	38.5
1995	10.3	39.5

Source: Kanoksak Kaewthep, *Wipark Tun Niyom Thai* (Bangkok: Chulalongkorn Book Centre, 1999), p. 17.

which is sufficient to plant rice for family consumption for one year. Since then the cost of fertilizer has increased, and the monsoon rain does not always come in the appropriate season. The economic crisis in the 1990s only exacerbated the situation. Social activist Nantiya Tangwisutijit writes, "The country's natural resources and the rural poor will be exploited on a greater scale as the government tries to deal with the economic crisis by boosting export competitiveness and foreign investment."[11] Thus begins the cycle of borrowing and loss.

Due to their lack of credit, farmers submit their land deeds in exchange for loans. Loan sharks collect up to 120 percent interest per year. Consequently, farmers watch their landholdings shrink, until one day the fields that their ancestors tilled and raked for decades are no longer theirs. Workers in their own fields, they till and rake for someone else on the very land they once owned. From landowners to field workers, they labor until they have lost everything. It is not uncommon for poor farmers to buy rice on credit in order to feed their families. A farmer in Ban Buak said, "Investing in farming means selling inheritance in order to have enough money to invest. The harder we work, the poorer we get. But we have to do it otherwise we will have nothing to eat."[12] This sense of despair is well expressed by a farmer in Ban Tak Dad, in Phichit Province:

> Some started with buying a machine for harvesting. Then because of sickness, development, advanced technology, fertilizer and because of the increased in population while resources are scarce, people have to compete for farmland. With increase in the rental price and drought, we are forced to take more loans, which means our interest keeps going up and so we are getting deeper and deeper into debt.[13]

Life's rewards seem so paradoxical, but perhaps not, if we understand that at some point in the national strategic development plan, cash became more important than crops. Again, this may not be the case. Perhaps we have allowed technology and economy to define our very essence. Hence, the "farmer became a sharecropper, then a peasant without land, then an agricultural laborer, then, eventually forced into exile."[14]

Tipa

While in Thailand, I came to know a number of these farmers and daily wage earners. Tipa, a thirteen-year-old girl, was born into one such family. Her parents are divorced. Her father lives in Bangkok, while she stays with her mother in the small village of Ban Tung Yen, in Phayao Province. Because of the level of poverty, Tipa's mother works odd jobs in the village. At the time of my visit, she worked peeling ginger, earning three baht (eight cents) per kilo. A full day's labor brought in an income of ten baht (twenty-five cents). In other seasons she might work planting rice or picking corn in the field. For that she earns seventy to eighty baht (two dollars) per day. In her letter (February 2001) to Clara and Johnny Ramirez, her sponsors who provided scholarship for her education, Tipa wrote, "I am so grateful for your help. Without your assistance I will never have a chance to go to school and continue with my education. I will use the money wisely and carefully."

Nong

Some poor village girls are not as lucky as Tipa. Nong supported her eleven-year-old daughter and thirteen-year-old son by working in the field as an agricultural laborer. She earns 100 baht per day when she can get work, but she never knows how often she will be called to work in the field. Her parents were very poor, and a few years ago her mother passed away. They have no land and live in a small hut out in the field. Everyone sleeps in the same room. When Nong was eighteen she got married, only to be abandoned nine months later. The next year she remarried to a soldier who, after giving her a son, disappeared from her life. At the age of twenty-one she remarried again. This husband was a drinker and lost his life through alcohol abuse, but he left her with a daughter. Without a husband, with minimal education, and with two children and an aging father to care for, she struggled in the field to earn whatever she could. Her situation just got harder when her children had to attend school. When a few village girls returned from southern Thailand with their savings to support their families, Nong accepted their invitation to work in a brothel in Sungai Golok. The brothel was run by Pa Kaen, and her working hours were usually from 8:00 a.m. to 1:00 a.m.

"We lived in a shop house in Sungai Golok. We all slept in one big room on the second floor. When customers come we have to go downstairs and sit in the waiting room. There are a red sofa and ten wooden chairs. Customers would walk around, examine, and pick their girls."

"What were you thinking while you were with customers?" I asked.

"I just wanted to be selected by a nice customer who would treat me well. I wanted someone to love and treat me well."

"How were you treated by customers?"

"They were usually very demanding. They paid for the service and expected me to do whatever they wanted me to do for them. Sometimes I just sat and cried in the motel room."

"What were you thinking when you stayed by yourself at the shop house?"

"I wanted badly to return home. I really missed home."

"Why didn't you visit home?"

"I did not feel like I was earning enough to help my family. I had to pay Pa Kaen. I had to pay rent. I had to pay taxi drivers who brought clients or introduced clients to me. By the time everything was deducted I had very little left."

"But you came back?"

"Yes. I was too homesick to stay on and decided to return home."

Nong came home, worked in the field, and remarried. Her new husband worked in a welding shop. He was an amphetamine addict. He sold everything he could find in the house and spent all the money she had earned on his addiction.

"We quarreled every day," she said, her voice filled with frustration and despair.

The last I heard, Nong's husband had shot himself in the head and she was considering returning to the south, and prostitution.

REFLECTION

Poverty plays an important role in making prostitution an attractive alternative. None of the girls I talked to would have chosen prostitution if not for their level of poverty. These questions remain: How do we define poverty? Is poverty the only factor that motivates these girls to offer their sexual services?

I pondered these questions as I strolled through the streets of Bangkok. My focus shifted to the Bangkok Transit System (BTS), a sky train that helped people beat Bangkok's congested traffic for seventy-five cents—convenient, fast, comfortable. I could be shopping downtown within a short time. I traveled well yet still complained about the Internet service—not that I could not get through, but that it was too slow. "It took me half an hour," I told a friend, "to read three e-mail messages in Chiang Rai." This technology is part of my everyday life, a normal part of my community, yet I can't help but wonder how much of this everyday technology downsizes farmlands, decreases agricultural products, and makes returning to the south an attractive option for Nong. How much of this everyday life has contributed to the life of buffalo boys who are "left only with the fabric of bygone days, Woven sight and sound of love before it all decays"?[15]

Chapter 4

Chiang Mai Restaurants:
Entering the Sex Trade

If a child remains sad,
How bad our future must be;
Let us, while time's to be had,
Brighten our children's smile!

Paiwarin Khao-Ngam
"Small Children in Big Cities"

I wonder, "Is poverty the only reason?" What about Tabtim's life? Was she really that poor? What was it like to grow up in that small village of Ban Pongnong? Sitting across from Tabtim in a café at Robinson Mall, I pulled out my notepad as I prepared to listen to her story.

"What is your earliest recollection of your life?" I asked.

Tabtim recalled an incident from when she was five years old and helping her mother with laundry. The event impressed her deeply because while she was scrubbing clothes her mother started yelling about all the mistakes and mess this five-year-old was making. She thought she was helping and found her mother's screaming confusing and disturbing.

Another early recollection was again while she was helping her mother with housework and was told to stop whatever she was doing. When Tabtim asked why, her mother just told her to wait for a pickup truck that sold cabinets. Tabtim was very excited. She wanted a place to store her belongings. The truck came and left but there was no cabinet. She remembered thinking that her mother had no intention of buying the cabinet. The intention was to get rid of her. The realization was frightening for a five-year-old. Nothing she did was ever good enough. Her description of these incidents reminded me of the day I met her mother at her residence. "Tell me something about Goung," I asked.

Tabtim's mother described her daughter as lazy, a girl who had no interest in helping with housework, a girl who was content to sit around doing nothing. To her mother, Tabtim only enjoyed going out with friends and returning home late at night, a girl who loved to socialize, listened only to her friends' advice, and disobeyed her parents.

Apparently Tabtim did not see herself the way her mother perceived her. After a brief moment of trying to process this information, I asked Tabtim what she liked to do when she was little, and learned that she hated being around many people. She enjoyed visiting her grandmother and hanging around her home. She had a few friends and loved to play with her second brother, jumping on his back and playing "horse". He made her laugh and brought sweets home for her during his lunch breaks from school. They played, laughed, and ate together until it was time for him to return to school. One day, he decided not to go back to school and hid himself between some bamboo bushes until school was over. His father found out, tied him to a bamboo bush, spanked him, and let red ants bite him. He never missed school from that day on.

Tabtim attended Anubarn Ban Nai Vieng School until she completed the sixth grade. While in school, she had two close friends, Yupa and Patchanee. Nothing exciting happened in her life except for one evening when she went swimming in a pond near her school with these friends and almost drowned. Her friends pulled her out and by the time she got home, it was late. She got spanked by her father.

Her favorite teacher was Kru Pongsri who always invited Tabtim to have lunch with her. While eating, she would tell stories about the importance of being good, about being morally upright, about honesty, and virtue. Those stories became Tabtim's inspiration. Goodness and virtue were a part of her educational experience. Tabtim recalled these experiences with fondness.

PARENTS

The unfolding of one's life is closely intertwined with one's primary caregivers, one's parents. I needed to know what Tabtim thought of her parents and what they were like during her formative years.

Tabtim said she was close to her father, whom she described as quiet and reasonable. She respected him and found him approachable. On many occasions, she had the opportunity to help him harvest rice in the field, but her relationship with her mother was the opposite.

She found it difficult to talk to her mother because normal conversations often turned into arguments. She described her mother as an unreasonable person who loved to scream at her children, someone who talked loudly and scolded without reason. Tabtim explained that her mother's behavior was a result of alcoholism. This also explained why Tabtim did not want to stay at home, why she was always at her grandmother's place, and why she usually returned home late in the evening. She did not want to see her drunk mother screaming at her father. On a number of occasions, Tabtim tried to intervene, but ended up being screamed at. It was her mother's alcoholism that made staying home a very unpleasant experience. As a little girl, she and her brother often sat holding each other, crying and wondering why their mother had to get drunk every night. Sometimes, her brother would take her to his friends' homes. He, too, escaped by visiting friends, singing, and playing guitars. These places were like a sanctuary to her broken spirit, a resting place before returning to strife and confusion.

The Thai newspapers in Los Angeles painted the picture of Tabtim as a drug addict, irresponsible, and unfit to be a mother. I heard remarks such as, "What kind of mother is she?" "How could she do this to her son?" One day, while visiting Got's paternal grandparents, Boonlue and Sumalee Khaisri, who came to Los Angeles to be with their grandson, I asked them about Goung.

"From what I've heard," said Boonlue, "she was one of those *jai tak* girls [spoiled teenager who is attracted to nightlife]. She spent lots of time with her friends. She did not want to study. She did not stay at home. She would return home late at night."

"How did she get involved in the sex industry?" I asked.

"One of her aunties who had previously been working in this business came home and invited her to go and work in Chiang Mai. She started working in a restaurant, which was also a bar. There she started entertaining clients."

Looking back at this conversation with Boonlue and having visited Tabtim's mother, I gather that she was Boonlue's source of information. What he learned about Tabtim was Yai Tong's judgment of her daughter, a judgment lacking in self-awareness. It is perhaps easier to construct a rationale to explain her daughter's behavior than to acknowledge her intoxication as the reason. It is easier to assume than to ask. That Tabtim is a *jai tak* girl is a safer assumption then pausing to ask, "Why do you come home late?" To ask is to risk knowing what one may not wish to acknowledge. Perhaps Yai Tong knew it all along. I often wonder why some people have such a difficult time admitting their mistakes. When one feels so wrong, it is harder to accept more wrongs. When one's shadow is overwhelming, the ego has to sever itself to maintain sanity. I wonder how much of this projected ego on the part of Yai Tong has been internalized by Tabtim.

LEAVING HOME

Tabtim was constantly searching for reasons to leave her family. She did not like what she saw at home. She hated the disturbing tension that comes with alcoholism, the screaming, swearing, and fighting. After completing her sixth grade education, her auntie invited her to Chiang Mai to work in her restaurant. It was one of those restaurants that doubled as a bar, serving clients who were looking for more than good food and intoxication. She worked weekdays and went to school on Sunday.

Chiang Mai was like a haven to her, a place free from strife and tension. There was no screaming, no swearing, and no fighting. She did not have to be reminded daily that she was not wanted. With a few friends, work, and school, two years passed by rather quickly. By the time she left, she was sixteen. She went to Bangkok where the work was very similar to what she did while in Chiang Mai. Tabtim worked in a similar type of restaurant located at Sukapibarn Nung for the following year and a half.

RESTAURANTS AND CAFÉS

I wonder what the phrase "working in a restaurant" means. Tabtim did not elaborate. According to research by the Faculty of Social Science, Chiang Mai University, restaurant and pub refers to a country-style restaurant with a variety of music. Customers sit in an open-air space with a bar counter to the side. Trees, plants, and shrubs are used to provide a natural setting. The front entrance is usually lit up with colorful lights. Young, good-looking girls wearing short skirts or pants with tight tops serve as waitresses. Owners of these restaurants often claim that they sell good food, sweet wine, and music, not sex. However, they all have a rule that girls must wear their uniforms or their pay will be cut or they will not receive their share of customers' tips. The uniform is a short skirt or pants and a tight spaghetti-strap top. They receive between 2,500 and 4,500 baht (US$65 to $100) per month. They work from 6:00 p.m. until midnight or 2:00 a.m. The main intention of girls who work here is not waiting on customers, but offering themselves for men's pleasure in exchange for money. Although sex is the goal, their approach is indirect. First-time customers will not receive an explicit sexual invitation but instead casual conversation and pleasant service. These girls will work on the relationship to the point at which the level of familiarity permits them to invite customers out for more drinks or to a disco. This is when negotiation for sex takes place. These girls earn 1,500 baht per night for sleeping with clients. Locations are varied: a motel or apartment, the girl's apartment, or the client's residence.[3]

Cafés are similar to restaurants, offering food, liquor, and sex services. Young girls lean against one another at the front; they often wear short skirts and numbers pinned to their shirts. The color of the number indicates the girl's price. A café is a brothel that serves food, beer, and liquor. Selling food and beer qualifies the business as a café, which helps to circumvent the laws regarding prostitution. Music, singers, dim light, liquor, and beer are what one encounters on entering the café. The second floor is divided into small rooms, an accommodation for pimps and prostitutes and for sexual services, after clients pay their fees at the counter. Most of the girls working in cafés are between fifteen and twenty years old. The majority are from northern Thailand or from the Thai Yai group.[4] Lessons on mixing liquors, pleasing clients, and tempting clients to order more liquor are taught upon hiring. Remuneration is a fifty-fifty deal: the girls get half, the café, the other half. If the girls get caught, however, that half will be subdivided until the fine is paid in full. Girls work a ten-hour shift, 6:00 p.m. until 4:00 a.m., but on weekends or special holidays, they are expected to work till 5:00 a.m. They are allowed to leave the café once a week but must return in the evening.

I used to think that prostitutes are lazy. They want quick money and an easy job. How hard can having sex be? I get paid for forty hours per week but usually work more hours than required. I consider myself to be hardworking. These girls work sixty hours a week, waiting, pleasing, seducing, and entertaining clients. Perhaps seducing motivated clients is not that difficult, but it may be more complex than we realize. They dress up to look pretty. At 6:00 p.m. they serve. Most clients do not spend too much time eating or drinking; they drink, negotiate, and have sex. Forty-five minutes is the maximum time given to undress and service a client. A quick shower and a girl is ready to pick up another client. When the café is congested, the pimp's advice is to "use your fingers, speed up the process." Speeding up is a good technique, since more clients mean higher income. The average price before midnight is 100 to 200 baht per session. After midnight, the price increases to 300 baht per visit. Normally each girl entertains five to ten clients per night. They have to be conscious of time while working the clients. Ten clients per night means one hour to pour drinks, pick up a condom, undress, entertain, take a shower, dress up, and get back on the floor. During festivals, each girl may have to entertain up to twenty clients per night.[5]

Although Tabtim worked in this type of restaurant, I had the impression that her self-perception was not one of a sex worker. She considered her contacts with clients in the context of love and relationship.

ENTERING THE SEX INDUSTRY

Although Tabtim grew up in a poor family, poverty was not the only contributing factor, and this applies to other cases as well. In their analysis of fifty children and teenagers who are working in different types of sex trade, Thai Women of Tomorrow found that forty-four out of fifty are girls and six are boys. In terms of age, six are below the age of fifteen, thirty-eight are between fifteen and eighteen, and six are nineteen years old. Family structures of these children may be divided as shown in Table 4.1.[6]

When Tabtim was fourteen, she just wanted to get out. She wanted to leave home. In fact, even when she was at home, she was not there. When she was elsewhere, she realized deep down that she did not really have a home: "I spent lots of time at my grandmother's place." A

TABLE 4.1. Family Structures of Fifty Children Who Entered the Sex Trade

Family Structure	Number	Percent
1. Good relationships	25	50
2. Conflicts in the family	6	12
3. Divorce in the family	15	30
4. Orphans	4	8

Source: Thai Women of Tomorrow, *Kabuan Karn Chak Joong Dek Kao Su A-cheep Kai Borikarn Tang Pedt* (Chiang Mai: Thai Women of Tomorrow, 2000).

place of refuge is not a home. Poverty certainly made things worse. In contrast to Tabtim, 50 percent of prostitutes came from families with good relationships. What then induced them into the sex industry? Poverty, education, mass media, lack of religious emphasis, and lack of clear policy on the part of the government to eliminate the problem of child prostitution are some contributing factors.[7]

Pornpan

A health coordinator in Ban Hui Kieng, in Chiang Rai Province, Mr. Hla Pramoonkong guided my friends and me to a wooden house off the main freeway. We waited at the front of the house and soon saw a young lady walking on a narrow path toward us. Her name was Pornpan, a thirty-two-year-old ex-prostitute. She was sweet-looking with a pleasant personality. We all sat on the cement floor and her mother brought each of us a cup of water. Pornpan had only a sixth-grade education. Her parents work in the field planting rice. They had less than ten rai. "We were very poor. Our monthly income was about 1,000 baht. With six of us in the family, I did not want to continue my education. I wanted to work in order to help support my family." Pornpan found a job working in a bakery in Chiang Rai. She started at 150 baht a month, but this increased to 500 baht. And because she was capable and hardworking, she soon got promoted to supervisor, despite her young age. One day while working with the bread-mixing machine, her right arm got caught and was almost torn apart.

"The injury was really bad, and when the arm was sewn back, it did not attach right. I cannot use my right arm like before. It is shorter than my left, and my fingers don't have the same grip like before the accident."

Pornpan paused a while. Her eyes turned red and filled with tears. She dried her tears, but her small hand could not erase the deep scars of sorrow. "It was a changing point in my life. I could not do the work that I used to do. I had no education."

She returned home and helped her parents for two years, working in the field and at home cleaning, cooking, and washing. Her friends came back from Bangkok and extended an invitation.

"I knew what I was getting into. I knew I had to provide sex in exchange for money. I made up my mind because my family was really poor. My first client bought my virginity for 5,000 baht."

Pornpan worked in a hotel on Prachatipratai Road entertaining three clients per night. After paying back the money she borrowed from the business owner, she returned home. Before the year was over, she heard about another working location that seemed, at that time, to provide better working conditions. She went to Nakhon Pathom, a city south of Bangkok. Here she would wait at her own residence. Hotel staff would call her when they had clients wanting to be gratified. A client paid 100 baht; she received 35 baht. Entertaining five to six clients per day, she was earning approximately 5,000 baht per month. Of course, she still had to pay the rent, electric bills, and phone bills, but this was better than 1,000 baht per month for an entire family. After two years she started working as a masseuse. The money was better; she received 50 baht an hour. If the client decided to "off" her, she could earn as much as 1,000 baht.

It was around this time, too, that she fell in love with a married man and lived with him as a minor wife for two years. Those two years dictated her final destiny. He was a womanizer. Soon after quitting this relationship, she fell ill and lost a lot of weight. Wiping the tears off her face, she said, "March 16 of 2000 I got the result back. It was positive for HIV."

Nid

Nid is about five feet four inches. Her long black hair is well groomed. Her complexion is on the darker side. Tight jeans and white top with light makeup made her look very presentable. Nid grew up in Udon Thani, a province northeast of Bangkok. Her father works in the field planting tapioca and sugar cane. She described her family as warm and loving. After completing her associate's degree in accounting she went to Bangkok to work at Maboonklong Center (MBK Center) in downtown Bangkok. She worked in the cosmetic section as a salesperson. After a year in Bangkok her friends invited her to join the sex industry.

"It took me a month to make that decision," she reflected.

"What made you decide to enter this business?" I asked.

"I owed money for my rent. Then at the end of the month I was still short of money for both months. I did not want to move out. I did not know where to move to. And my friend kept calling me mentioning good clients."

"What was it like the first time you were with a client?"

"It was hard having sex with a stranger. I felt conflicted. I forced myself to be pleasant. I guess what helped me was the fact that I had had sexual relations with my boyfriend before entering this business."

"Who are your customers?"

"Businessmen, bankers, mostly married men who are financially well established."

"Have you changed since engaging yourself in this business?"

"I feel like I am not a good person anymore. I have to mix with a different social group. I now socialize with girls who are in the same business because I feel like a bad person when I'm with other groups."

"What runs through your mind when you are by yourself?"

"Many girls are doing what I'm doing. I'm not alone here. I'm not materialistic. I'm not bad. There are other girls with bachelor's degrees doing this same thing. They are the ones who are materialistic. I work and I send money home."

Nid has a dream. Her dream is to open a small dress boutique—to sell dresses instead of sex. For now she will continue to see clients until the shop can help her become financially independent.

"When will that happen?" I asked.

"I don't know if it ever will," she replied.

REFLECTION

Although it is not possible to draw a generalization regarding the reasons young girls enter the sex industry, the three stories presented in this chapter do convey a certain pattern. While for Tabtim poverty was not the only issue, it was certainly true for the others. Both Pornpan and Nid did not experience conflicts in their families. Nid, however, had an associate's degree from a public college in her province. She migrated to Bangkok and found herself a job as a salesperson. However, her pay could not cover her rent and other related expenses. Nid's engagement in prostitution did not offer a luxurious lifestyle. She offered this type of service only twice a month, which earned her approximately 2,000 baht.

One question comes to mind when we hear stories of young girls volunteering themselves: Can't they work harder or live more simply instead of choosing prostitution? Perhaps.

Nari grew up helping her parents weave baskets to sell in Chiang Rai. Their daily wage was 30 baht. She lived in a small bamboo hut at the edge of the village of Bo Tong with five other siblings and her parents. Now there are only five in the family; her three brothers died of AIDS. They were very poor. After completing grade six, she went south and sold her body in Sungai Golok to support her family. When she tired of the south, she returned to Chiang Rai and worked in a brothel. She is now twenty-six. "I feel pretty good about myself." Nari was diagnosed with HIV eight years ago. After spending much of her hard-earned money on medication, she is now living with her parents and weaving baskets.

Perhaps she should have stayed home and weaved baskets. She would have been poor but healthy. Sixteen years ago in her village, who would have thought that prostitution could be deadly? Nari did not think so, and she headed south to avoid spending the rest of her life weaving baskets. Was she a consumerist for wanting something better? I found it difficult to answer this question. Perhaps the glamour of the mass media gradually intensified her desire for something better. Still, all the glamour would not have made any difference if the means were not made available: Men were out there and willing to pay for sex, a demand seeking a supply. This type of demand has destroyed many young lives. We are reminded of Khao-Ngam's concern:

> Too many youngsters suffer ills,
> Trampled by their adults;
> And the world ne'er fulfills
> Their crippled hope for kindness.[8]

Chapter 5

Rickshaw Driver: Paying for Sex

On the chest full of current scars
A crimson rain of blood runs foul,
While milky tears of eternal stars
Erode the stony ledge of our soul.

Paiwarin Khao-Ngam
"The Flame and the Dreamer"

Discussing the role of tourism and its impact on child prostitution in Thailand, Jeremy Seabrook, in *No Hiding Place,* writes:

The expansion of travel and vacations, journeys and holidays have made tourism the largest single industry on earth. It is inevitable that among the vast number of people traveling to the Third World, some will go with purposes less honourable than the pleasure of traveling. In the mid-1990s, when about six million people visited Thailand annually, almost two-thirds of these were single males. Among them, it is only to be expected that some were attracted by the relative ease with which underage young people might be procured for sexual purposes.[1]

It was 10:00 p.m. I was walking back to Wangcome Hotel in Chiang Rai. Just before crossing a narrow lane leading to a hotel, a rickshaw driver greeted me. He must have been fifty or older. Wrinkles on his tanned face and rugged complexion told stories of a body beaten by summer heat and monsoon rain, bending in rice fields, maneuvering buffalo. Leaning against his colorful tricycle smoking a cigarette, he smiled, revealing nicotine marks on his teeth.

"You want a girl?" he asked, an offer he makes to tourists late in the night.

I smiled, thinking to myself, "He should have good information."

"They are gorgeous and young."

"How young?" A research question of interest to me.

"Very young . . . high school age. And they are very pretty. Come on. Get into my rickshaw and I will show you."

I was tempted to pass by the place just to take a look. But since I had to get up very early the next morning I decided not to. "Who are these girls anyway?"

"They are mostly from Burma and China."

"How do they manage to come all the way to Chiang Rai?"

"Well, they mostly have a special pass that permits them to come as far as Chiang Rai but no farther. Come on. Get in here and I will show you."

"It's okay. I have to leave early tomorrow morning. But do you go visit these girls too?"

"Of course not. They are too expensive. I can't afford that."

"But if you could, would you?"

"Definitely. If someone pays for me I will go for sure."

"You are not afraid of AIDS?"

"I'm old. I'm going to die anyway. What've I got to lose?"

I learned that taxi drivers, rickshaw drivers, and pickup drivers in northern Thailand are wonderful resources for nightlife. Similar to salespeople who have to know their products to earn extra income, these people are constantly being asked by tourists where to go for exciting entertainment and what options are available, including price range. These drivers can make recommendations to clients according to clients' taste and income level. They earn a portion of their livelihood making recommendations to clients thirsting to gratify basic sexual needs. Occasionally prostitutes or pimps pay them when they deliver clients.

With demand, there will always be supply. The question remains: Who uses the services of these young girls? I believe three main types of perpetrator take advantage of young girls: old Chinese men (old cows chewing young grass), pedophiles, and Thai men in general.

TYPES OF PERPETRATORS

Old Cows Chewing Young Grass

Bold letters on the front page of the *Bangkok Post,* January 22, 2001, read "Chalerm sought over sex claims: Senator accused of romp with minor": "Police are preparing to summon Deputy Senate Speaker Chalerm Promlert to answer allegations he had sex in a motel with four schoolgirls, including a minor."[2] Mr. Chalerm was charged for spending two days with students aged thirteen to sixteen at a motel in Pathum Thani's Lam Looka district and paying them 4,000 baht each. These girls were brought to Mr. Chalerm by a seventeen-year-old girl who is a school dropout.

A mother of one of the victims, a fourteen-year-old, stormed into Klonghluang Police Station in Pathum Thani Province, charging Senator Chalerm Promlert with buying sex from young girls. The incidents took place on December 22, 2000, and January 3, 2001. The girls were brought to rooms 231 and 232 at Phaga In Motel in Pathum Thani. According to police reports, Chalerm used pornography to induce desire before having sexual intercourse with each girl. The girls reported that each session did not last that long; on the first day, Chalerm checked in at 9:00 a.m. and checked out at 11:00 a.m., and on the second day, he checked in at 4:00 p.m. and checked out at 6:00 p.m.[3] Yongyut Wongpiromsarnt of the Mental Health Department, Ministry of Health, told reporters that this type of behavior is called "Old cows chewing on young grass." Its roots lie in the misconception that having sex with young girls will provide health, longevity, and sexual prowess.[4] Such news makes one wonder about the level of depravity in Thailand's society. Of course, the senator denied the charges, claiming that he was framed. We do not really know the truth. If it is true that this senator was having sex with four kids between the ages of thirteen and sixteen, we cannot help but wonder what sickness this is. According to Yongyut Wongpiromsarnt, this is not pathological. It is a misconception. It becomes pathological when a person seeks an even younger population.

Pedophiles

An American survey of sex abusers found that 67,000 children were victims of 403 pedophiles. Each pedophile victimized, on an av-

erage, 283 children in his or her lifetime.[5] Of course, extreme cases
do exist. An Australian court recorder working for juvenile offenders,
Clarence Osborne, molested 2,500 boys during his lifetime. Police
discovered detailed records and photos of his activities.

Thailand is one of the sex tour destinations for pedophiles. Jeremy
Seabrook reports a typical case in Thailand in his book *No Hiding
Place:*

> On 18 May 1998, the Correctional Tribunal in Bruges convicted
> Marc Boonen, a 48-year-old unmarried teacher, of unlawful
> sexual contact with a child aged under 16 years in Thailand.
> This was the second conviction of a Belgian national for sex
> tourism, and the first one under the new extraterritorial law of
> 1995. Boonen was arrested early in the evening of 16 July 1996
> in a hotel room in Pattaya with a 14-year-old boy. Both were
> naked. Boonen had arrived in Thailand two weeks earlier. He
> had met the victim several days before his arrest. He had bought
> clothes for him, and invited him to his hotel room to take a
> shower and then to watch television.[6]

In 1990 an undercover Australian police officer infiltrated a pedophile club in Melbourne and found eight men preparing to visit a
number of pedophile clubs in Thailand. Each of them had been to
Thailand before, and one of them had had sex with 250 children. Figure 5.1 shows the distribution of convicted pedophiles by nationality.[7]

In a small hotel located at the edge of Chiang Mai, a group of men
meet regularly once a month. They call themselves the Blues Club.
They have passion. They have purpose. They care for one another and
always share news and information. They are respectable citizens,
model members of society, conservative in their religious views and
political outlook. They meet in secret—even their own family members remain unaware. Their secret is that they love young boys with
passion.

Jake, a member of the Blues Club, informed his group about the
publication *A Survival Manual.* They do not know who wrote it. The
book starts with information on the right place, the right room, and
the right time to have sex. It contains many exciting stories of sex in
unusual places, the tricks used to lure boy lovers, what happens if
they are arrested, how to avoid serious charges (by plea-bargaining

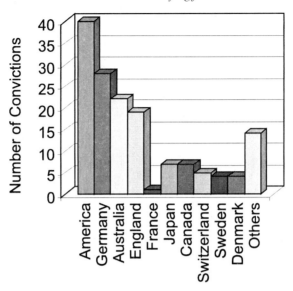

FIGURE 5.1. Convicted Pedophiles in Thailand by Nationality from 1991-1994: A Random List (*Source:* Ron O'Grady, *The Rape of the Innocent: One Million Children Trapped in the Slavery of Prostitution,* Auckland: ECPAT International, 1994, p. 137. *Note:* This list does not include all convictions; it reports only those which were of significant news value, the 160 convictions.)

without implicating your friends), and, in case of imprisonment, how to survive attack by prisoners and wardens.

Jake's favorite portion of the book is on becoming a fugitive when things really go wrong. The book discusses how to open a bank account under a false name, how to collect from different credit cards under assumed names, how to rent without tying up money in property, and how to keep traveler's checks in a safe deposit box for a quick getaway.

Thai Men

A seven-year research project by Nongphanga Limsuwan, of Ramathibodi Hospital's Mental Health Science Department shows that "[a]t least 25% of Thai men are polygamous, particularly during the ages of 30-50." This study is based on her interviews with eighty men in Bangkok.[8] The reasons for having a minor wife or wives are

(1) failure in their family life, (2) failure to view polygamy as morally wrong, and (3) intention at the outset to have more than one wife (see Table 5.1).

According to Chitraporn Vanaspongse of ECPAT, Thai men are the main consumers for sexual services by young girls.

Other Types of Perpetrators

Of course many types of child sexual abusers exist. The discussion of differential diagnosis of child sexual abusers by Kathleen C. Faller in her book *Child Sexual Abuse: An Interdisciplinary Manual for Diagnosis, Case Management, and Treatment* offers a number of categories. "In classical incest, the interaction between the father and daughter begins as appropriate affectionate physical behavior that gradually becomes sexualized, with the father perhaps initiating caressing of the child's perineal area."[9] In most cases, sexual contact starts at the oedipal stage (three to five years) and progresses to more intrusive forms of sexual behavior, such as mutual masturbation, oral/genital sex, and sometimes genital intercourse. There is also a stranger child rapist who may have assaulted many children but has only a single sexual encounter with a given child, with no gradual progression as in the classical incest cases. "A stranger suddenly grabs a child from his car or pulls a child into an alley. The sexual abuse itself is more likely to involve penetration than in incest and force is more often used."[10]

Psychopathologies that contribute to child sexual abuse include psychosis, mental retardation, and pedophilia. Psychosis constitutes only 2 percent of the sample Faller gathered. Common features of delusion among schizophrenics are persecution and grandiosity.[11] "Perpetrators often appear to deal with their own libidinous feelings, which are out of control, by projecting them onto others or the environment, while at the same time justifying their own sexual behavior."[12] An example cited was a mother who feared that the FBI and U.S. Government were trying to get devil worshipers to sexually molest her daughter. She counteracted by giving her daughter enemas and inserting her fingers into the girl's vagina.

Mentally retarded perpetrators are rare. It is common to learn that their perverted sexual predisposition originated from their being victimized at an earlier age. Hence, when they become adolescents or

TABLE 5.1. Rationales for Having a Minor Wife or Wives in Thailand

Reasons	Percentage
1. Failure in family life	10
2. Not morally wrong to have more than one wife	35
3. Intended to have more than one wife from the outset	55

adults, they assume the aggressor role. Their lack of opportunity for appropriate relationships contributes to the risk of inappropriate sexual acting out.[13] All pedophiles in Faller's sample had sexual encounters as children. Perpetrators also tend to identify with the children they are abusing. Children are most often of the same sex as the perpetrators and of an age that approximates the age the perpetrators were first victimized. The sexual acts often mimic what the perpetrators experienced.[14]

Perhaps it is difficult to understand what goes on in the thought process of those who abuse children. Faller offers two prerequisites for child sexual abusers: (1) sexual feelings toward children and (2) willingness to act upon sexual feelings toward children (the domain of the superego). A person with mild sexual feelings toward children and a poor superego is a prime candidate for perpetrating sexual abuse. A person with similar feelings and a strong superego will not. However, an individual with intense feelings toward children stands a good chance of giving in to these sexual urges even with a strong superego.[15]

Assessment of perpetrators' superegos, based on 175 samples, indicates that 6.9 percent have a strong superego, 16 percent have a moderate superego, 17.7 percent have a somewhat impaired superego, 37.1 percent have an impaired ego, and 22.3 percent have none.[16]

THE MARKET

Marketing operates by the law of supply and demand. A market for the sex industry exists because men are willing to pay for sexual services. What actually takes place, however, is more complicated than this relationship between demand and supply.

While on the Rama IV road heading toward Thonburi, Busarin "Pat" Wareesangtip, a close friend who helped me with the research, phoned a friend of hers for information on prostitutes. Twenty minutes later we got a call back. Her friend gave us a phone number: "Contact her. She is a *nok tor,* and she will arrange an interview for you." *Nok tor,* I learned later, refers to an agent with a list of ladies who are willing to provide sexual services for money. There is no central office. Negotiation is done over the phone. When all is set, a *nok tor* will take the girl to the appointed location, collect the money, and leave the girl with the client. In most cases, the girl earns 1,000 baht and the agent, 500.

I could not hear what this *nok tor* was saying to Pat, but I could hear Pat negotiating with her. She negotiated well.

"How much do you charge? . . . Give us a good rate. . . . We are not going to have sex. We just want to ask her questions, and answering questions is much easier than having sex. . . . How about a thousand? . . . Thank you. We will see you at ten p.m."

We went to a run-down apartment and walked up to the fourth floor. A lady in her thirties stood in a dark corridor with a young girl waiting for us. We entered a tiny two-bedroom apartment and were invited to sit on a beat-up red-vinyl couch. This *nok tor* was fair complexioned, a nice-looking lady who, we learned later, had worked as a prostitute herself about a decade ago. Now she entertains only some very special clients.

"I have three hundred women on my list," the *nok tor* told us.

"Where do they come from?" Pat asked.

"They are from all walks of life."

"How did they get into this business in the first place?" I asked.

"Some of them are *jai tak* girls who are lured by sights, sounds, and conveniences. Others were raped or sexually molested by their siblings, fathers, or stepfathers before joining this business. They figure that since they have lost what is most valuable to them, perhaps they should gain from it."

"Who are your clientele?"

"We have many policemen, government officials, military personnel, and businessmen. They are mostly well-established people."

"Do your clients request young girls, very young girls?"

"Some clients will specifically request young girls, but these are the minority, probably about two percent of my clientele. This is rare.

Clients have their own idiosyncratic tastes. Some will specify girls from a particular educational institution. Some ask for nurses. Some ask for married women. They have strange ideas, but I can always supply."

I was expecting to hear a much higher number than 2 percent, since the supply is plentiful. This only confirms what I heard from Chitraporn Vanaspongse of ECPAT International. Most Thai men do not specifically request young girls. Most of them are not pedophiles. They are made an offer and cannot resist the temptation of a new experience.

"However, there were cases," said Vanaspongse, "where when these men were in a room, they found a girl much younger than expected. The girls cried and these men reported to the Center for the Protection of Children's Rights and the police."

The information gathered from this *nok tor* and Vanaspongse is very disturbing. I do not really know what to make of it. It appears as if there are many young girls out there in this industry even though the demand may not be as great. If this is true, this tragic situation has, in a way, moved passed the law of supply and demand. Thus, we cannot help but wonder where we have gone wrong with all the lessons on virtues we learned from our parents about giving, sharing, loving, and creating a safe world for our children.

THE VICTIMS

That the supply of young girls in the sex industry is greater than the demand is very disturbing. If this is the case, why are young girls offering themselves to males for the purpose of sexual gratification? Perhaps there are multiple factors involved. Some girls leave their families because of tension and conflicts. Other girls want a better lifestyle, better education, or a better opportunity in life. Poor girls seek a way to support their families. Sisters want to provide education for their siblings, and mothers seek to support their children. Many young girls come to Thailand because they cannot survive financially in their own countries.

All these wants seem so normal, yet the path to obtain these basic needs and wants for these young girls seems so arduous, with limited alternatives and resources. Prostitution becomes the avenue to quick revenues and a more decent lifestyle. Most alarming is that more and more young girls think of the sex industry as an opportunity to acquire material goods and thus upgrade their lifestyle. Why are more young girls striving to upgrade their lifestyle? Poverty is more widespread, and the gap between rich and poor is bigger. The girls feel poorer, and the mass media tell them that what they have is undesirable. Stable job opportunities are scarce, but men are willing to pay for sex, and some people will do anything, including taking advantage of young girls, for their own success and prosperity.

Most heartbreaking are the stories of young girls who, after pursuing their dreams of prosperity through prostitution, find themselves having to spend their savings on medications for deadly diseases such as AIDS. Their dreams have become their worst nightmares. They are transformed from an object of desire into an object of scorn. Their poverty now is not about what they lack, but who they are. When destiny abandons them at the pit of despair, where do they go from there?

Chapter 6

Chiang Rai: Returning Home

With chest scars and a bleeding pain,
I must flee this chaos infernal,
And ride back o'er rice fields again
To beg for blessings paternal.

Paiwarin Khao-Ngam
"Banana Tree Horse I"

To "ride back o'er rice fields" is a common journey of young girls in the flesh market. Why do these young girls return home after all that they have experienced? Perhaps something about home—mother and father, brothers and sisters—affects the very essence of who they are. When they are forced to face who they are in their final stage, they have to "ride back o'er rice fields" to reassess their essence and reconstruct their sense of self.

"Because they are so young and so vulnerable, they get infected very easily. Once infected they return home," said a social worker in Phayao Province, describing children in prostitution to me.

"What happens when they arrive home?"

"Their parents usually build a small hut for them and visit them occasionally, bringing food and stuff. They live in isolation."

When a home is not a home, the soul aches.

For Tabtim, the one person who made her feel at home was dying—her older brother, Kob. Both of her brothers became infected, as do most men in the north who pay for sex, only to get more than they bargained for. Lacking knowledge of such an epidemic, they could not imagine how such intense pleasure could be deadly. It was deadly, however, and by the time they realized, it was too late.

THE FAMILY

Tabtim left her job at the restaurant in Bangkok and returned to Chiang Rai to care for her brother Kob, who was in the final stage of AIDS. She did not know then that she, too, was already infected. She was eighteen and it was Valentine's Day. A festival was under way at the hot spring approximately fifteen kilometers from her place. She went. Wiwat saw her and gave her a rose with an attached phone number. He came to see her a couple of times before they started dating. A month later they got married.

Tabtim told me that, initially, she did not like him.

I was a little puzzled hearing this statement. How is it possible to marry someone without liking that person? Perhaps wanting to be loved is not quite the same as loving. Considering that she was deprived of affection in her family, it is perhaps not difficult to understand how Tabtim was drawn to what appeared to offer her a chance of fulfillment. What one lacks, one may crave.

Soon after the wedding, they began to fight. I wanted to learn more about Wiwat. What was he like? Who was Wiwat from Tabtim's view? Her recollection offered the description of a man with a bad temper who was highly irritable. Everything seemed to be all about him, his life, his career, his comfort, his desires. They often fought over money because he could not hold a job and spent most of his time at her parents' place. He spent her hard-earned savings and loaned money to his friends. When confronted, he became very angry. He was not interested in changing nor was he planning to do anything about it. Tabtim learned to accept her situation, to keep everything on the inside. Drinking became his daily occupation and the consumption increased during the last year of their marriage.

Her description of Wiwat reminded me of my conversation with his father Boonlue Khaisri. "My son had difficulty keeping jobs. He moved from place to place. It made him very frustrated. But somehow he just could not get going. His three other siblings are doing very well in their careers and succeeding."

We talked for nearly an hour about his son, and Boonlue's description made me wonder whether Wiwat had attention deficit or impulse control disorder. Tabtim did not know the meaning of impulse control or attention deficit. She knew only that her frustration was real.

At fourteen Tabtim left home, a home she described as stormy, where her mother drank every day and her parents fought, a home where she could not have a conversation with her mother without getting into a fight: "She likes to scream at me." "O'er the rice fields" she returned to the very same home from which she had once escaped.

A couple of months after her marriage, Tabtim became pregnant. Through the advice of a district nurse who was aware that Tabtim was among an at-risk population, Tabtim took a blood test and learned that she was HIV positive. She was instructed by her physician not to breast-feed. I learned later, toward the end of the interview, that her previous boyfriend had infected her. For several months, she was deeply affected by the diagnosis. Her mood changed and sadness permeated her daily activities. Her detached method of coping led to numbness. On top of her struggle with this infection, the frequency of family conflicts intensified. The anger that Tabtim once internalized had reached a different level. It gained a voice and strength. The weary soul was no longer able to keep it buried. Even Tabtim did not recognize herself. It was not like her to scream and throw things around, but she had an explanation. She thought of herself as a person who believed in full commitment to love. Nevertheless, love had its limits and when one crossed those limits, love could never be regained. That was Tabtim's explanation of her feelings and behavior.

"Can you tell me something about the incident surrounding the death of Wiwat?" I inquired. "What I heard from newspapers, your mom, and your in-laws was that he found out that he was HIV positive and that led him to commit suicide."

What I learned from Tabtim was different from what I had previously heard. The night before he committed suicide, they had a fight. He went back to his parents' place and stayed overnight. The next morning he returned. They fought again about the fact that he could not hold a job, and his inability to provide for the family. Things got really ugly and in that moment of anger she told him that she wanted out of their marriage. Quietly, he packed his things, and as he approached the door, he turned and said to Tabtim, "Please take good care of my son." That evening, Tabtim received a call from Wiwat's mother, Sumalee.

Sumalee Khaisri recalled the incident. "I was working at the back of my house taking care of mushrooms. When I returned to the house through the garage, I saw his body hanging from a robe tied to the ceiling. It was too late."

Tabtim was numb during the funeral. She was not sad. She was not angry. She was not able to feel at all. Perhaps it was because the relationship had been so stormy, was her explanation.

THE PSYCHE

According to the Foundation for Women, Thailand, returning home is a common phenomenon. To some, it is the last place of refuge. When illness cripples one from socializing and then from mobilizing, home is still the place where family obligation makes possible accommodation and some warmth, at least. To others, it is the destination determined by one's psyche. It creates a drive for self-worth, when the inner self becomes aware of the outer filth from having multiple sex partners in exchange for cash. One seeks to validate oneself in the midst of one's sense of moral degeneration.

One prostitute described her feelings:

> I feel bad all the time. It is a type of job that is being looked down upon by societies. When we return home, our old friends who did not enter such trade look at us in a knowing way. I constantly struggle with a sense of inferiority. I'm afraid they will dislike me, and so I try not to mix around too much. We are not like our friends anymore. We have become impure. If we go out with them and their parents come to hear, we will be criticized. They will think that we try to lead their kids in the wrong direction. Sometimes I'm afraid even to have a good conversation with my own nieces. We do not wish to mix around anymore. People may say nice things to us but we do not know what they really think about us.[1]

This inner focus on the souls on these girls enhances our understanding of Nid's statement: "Many girls are doing what I'm doing. I'm not alone here. I'm not materialistic. I'm not bad . . . I work and I send money home." This speaks to the intrapsychic need of each individual for value and worth. Rahab the prostitute saved her entire family from the massive destruction in Jericho through her generosity. For Tabtim and others in her situation, returning home and improving their families' condition is the way to achieve justification, even self-redemption. It is most honorable to sacrifice for the family, even if it means sacrificing one's moral principles. Returning to rebuild their houses, with brick walls and new roofs, is all part of the restoration of the self. It helps to validate one's worth and to justify one's acts. For Tabtim, having her marriage fall apart right in front of her parents and her spouse lend her hard-earned money to others must have been very frustrating to her psyche—like watching whatever is left of oneself be flushed away, that very last hope for a meaningful self.

ACQUIRED IMMUNODEFICIENCY SYNDROME

Besides the psyche there is the body. Similar to Nari, who returned to weave baskets while watching her body waste away, many former prostitutes return home to die. Jan was nineteen when she returned to Wieng Pa Pao, to her house a couple of blocks from Tabtim's. She was just skin and bones and could hardly move. Jan was in pain. We later learned that she was in the final stage of AIDS. She left home when she was twelve, headed south, and started working in a restaurant earning 1,500 baht per month. After three months of hesitation, she began selling her body to lustful clients. She could not pinpoint when she got infected, but she kept working until she was too sick to work. The only place left to go then, when her body was no longer of any monetary value, was home.

According to reports by the public health department, in Chiang Rai Province, between 1988 and 2000, 11,994 people were diagnosed with AIDS. Of this figure, 4,084 passed away. In addition, 5,574 villagers are HIV positive and 449 are deceased. Hence, the total number of AIDS and HIV victims is 17,568 with 4,533 deaths (see Tables 6.1 and 6.2).[2]

In 1991 it was reported that approximately 50 percent of women from Chiang Rai and Phayao Provinces (northern Thailand) working in brothels and 30 percent of men attending sexually transmitted disease (STD) clinics were infected.[3] In 1999 there were 266 AIDS patients in Wieng Pa Pao District, the district where Tabtim grew up.[4] Discussing the AIDS epidemic in Thailand, Chris Lyttleton, an anthropologist from Macquarie University, Australia, wrote:

> Rates of transmission via heterosexual sex increased from 5.1% of new cases in 1988 to 46.9% in 1990. By 1996, heterosexual

contact was considered to account for roughly 80% of the AIDS caseload of which 12% were female and 67% male. Recent television PSAs [public service announcements] echo the message that almost 90% of AIDS cases come from sexual contact. Perhaps more revealing than the actual figures are the trends they depict. In a comparative estimate of HIV infection using data from women reporting to prenatal clinics and conscripted army recruits the ratio of male to female HIV infected cases dropped from roughly 9:1 in 1990 to 2.5:1 in 1993. In other words, in those three years many more women than men became infected. This trend is expected to sooner or later render infection levels equal between men and women.[5]

Housewives and Orphans

The equal gender distribution of infection means AIDS is no longer confined to prostitutes and their clients. Mothers and housewives

TABLE 6.1. AIDS Victims in Chiang Rai Province by Age

Age	Number	Percentage
<15	1,118	6.36
15-29	7,732	44.01
30-34	4,046	23.03
35-39	2,199	12.52
40-44	1,153	6.56
>45	1,320	7.52

TABLE 6.2. AIDS Victims in Chiang Rai Province by Occupation

Occupation	Number	Percentage
Farmer	8,242	46.92
Daily Wage Earner	5,508	31.35
Student	1,017	5.79
Business Owner	599	3.41
Housewife	584	3.32
Other	1,618	9.21

are now being infected. Noi Saikan, a villager in Chiang Rai told us that "most men do not go visiting prostitutes in brothels anymore. They are afraid. There are too many people dying a cruel death because of AIDS." The problem, as he sees it, is the many orphans created by men who visit prostitutes, become infected, and then infect their wives. Som is one of these orphans.

Som, a thirteen-year-old boy from Fang district in Chiang Mai, expressed his impression of the AIDS epidemic:

> AIDS kills a great number of people. There is AIDS in my village. I don't want to see people dying of AIDS or contracting it because they will be despised by others. My mum and dad both died of AIDS. Even though I can control my grief I never want to see anyone else get it again. I will protect myself. I won't go whoring. . . . I usually walk [to school] although some days I use my uncle's motorbike. My friends at school used to make fun of me for what happened to my parents, but I didn't get angry or pay it any mind since lots of kids around have the same type of problem. People with AIDS have spots on their bodies.[6]

Som may not wish to see people die of AIDS, but this is just a wish. He will witness many more deaths in his village. He will live long enough to see more children become orphans, to see children die young because they are infected at birth. The UNICEF Office in Thailand reports that 30,000 children are now orphans because of AIDS. In the next few years this number may climb as high as 200,000.[7]

In Ban Nong Bua Ngen, I met Weerachai, a four-year-old HIV-positive boy. His mother passed away in 1998, and his father, in 2000. Symptoms of AIDS appeared in his mother just before she gave birth to him. Right now he lives with his grandmother, who is taking care of five orphans, her grandchildren. She chops wood in the forest and sells it in the market. On a normal day she earns 30 baht, but if she is lucky she may earn up to 60 baht.

We do not know how much awareness Weerachai has regarding his condition. Nang, however, does know. Her husband, In, is now blind and in intense pain. He has been experiencing symptoms of AIDS for over one year. In 1998 he took a blood test and learned that he was HIV positive. Nang and In were married six years ago, and they have always travelled together. They went to Bangkok to work as construction workers together, and then south to work in a fishing village together. They have two children, a two-year-old and a seven-year-old. When she first heard this demoralizing news, she was paralyzed by fear and anger, intense anger. Then her anger turned to sorrow.

"After hearing the news did you have difficulty sleeping or have nightmares?"

"I had some. This is so unexpected." Her eyes turned red and filled with tears. "I did not think it would ever happen to me. I live a good life. I have never been promiscuous. I have a husband. I have my children. I work hard. And for all that I have done, this is what I got. There are promiscuous women selling sex who do not get infected. Why must this happen to me?"

"Has suicide ever entered your mind?"

"Definitely. There were times when we had nothing to eat, when we went hungry, that I thought of suicide. In the past one year my husband could not work. There were days when we had to spend money on his medications and did not have enough left for food. And there were days when I did not get a call to go work in the field. It was hard watching my little boy go hungry. I thought of suicide but I need to carry on for the sake of my children."

"When you observe your husband, has it ever occurred to you that you will go through this same process?"

"I thought about it. The thought of it really scares me. I have seen people in the final stage. They are in so much pain and they really look pathetic, and I thought, this is what I will be like when the time comes."

I stood watching her tears then turned to look at the little boy standing beside her.

I asked her, "Do you have a plan?"

As I listened to her reply I saw something deeper than sorrow.

"When I get to the stage when I become helpless, I will take my two kids to a foundation that cares for children whose parents die of AIDS." Her lips trembled and her voice quivered at the thought of parting from her children, at the thought of them as orphans. "Then I will go to a temple in Lopburi, a temple that takes care of AIDS patients."

In the words of Kahlil Gibran, "her mother died, leaving her nothing save tears of distress and the abasement of orphanhood."[8] Dying of AIDS is a terrifying thought, but the thought of one's children becoming orphans in a strange foundation is worse. Nang wondered about justice: How could choosing hard work over prostitution, poverty instead of quick money, turn her children into orphans? She also must wonder about the future of her son, which will be discovered when she has enough courage to take her son for the blood test.

For some children, the future is in their dreams. For others, the future is only a dream. Nik, a twelve-year-old girl from Lumphun Province, has a dream:

> The home of my dreams has trees all around and a mountain stream flowing by. In the morning the sun shows its smile and a flock of birds flies off in search of food. I live with my grandmother. My mum and my younger sister live in another house. My mum used to sell noodles, but she doesn't do it anymore. She was upset by the owner of another shop who said to people "don't buy noodles from her or you'll get AIDS." After that mum went to work on a building site. She had my uncle look after the kids. I've got an older sister who lives with my dad. My parents have broken up so I'm separated from my older sister. I was still very young when this happened. My parents remarried and I had to go and stay with my grandmother. I'm not sure whether mum has AIDS or not, but my older sister told me that she is infected. It doesn't bother me if mum has AIDS. I'd like to keep studying at school but I don't know if mum has enough money to support me. I'd like to be a doctor.[9]

This is Nik's dream. Her reality, however, is that without help from outside, Nik will most likely stop going to school by the time she is fourteen. There can be no prediction as to her future in the face of such poverty and limited education. The alternatives are scarce. According to an AIDSnet staff member who is aware of her situation, Nik's mother asked her eldest daughter to talk to her father about caring for Nik when she dies. He refused. Rejected, Nik has never returned to visit her father. Relatives believe that his refusal was due to his fear that Nik had caught the virus from her mother.[10]

Nik has a dream. Her future is in her dream. Some of us know better. We know that, as it is, her future is just a dream. But perhaps not. Perhaps her dream can be her future, if we have the courage to dream dreams.

> Where are you, my dreamer, tonight?
> Go heighten your consciousness,
> Then add colours, sound and light,
> O'er the real image of hideousness.[11]

Chapter 7

Somsak Deema: Trafficking Women and Children

> Lonesome in the age of modernity;
> Lonely in the epoch of emptiness;
> Lovelorn in the era of frivolity;
> Lost in the hour of hopelessness.
>
> Paiwarin Khao-Ngam
> "Banana Leaf Maiden"

April 11, 2000, Suseno Karjopranoto and Chu Mwei Long arrived at the Los Angeles International Airport (LAX) with a three-year-old boy, Somsak Deema. They were a family on vacation visiting Los Angeles—at least that was what they wished people to think. Somsak Deema was actually Phanupong Khaisri and Suseno Karjopranoto and Chu Mwei Long, a Chinese lady from Fujian Province, were no couple:

> Phanupong, nicknamed "Got," arrived . . . with a couple posing as sightseeing parents. When questioned . . . Karjopranato admitted that he and Chu Mwei Long were not married and that the boy was not his son.[1]

The couple was sent back to Thailand. The little boy was taken into custody of the U.S. Immigration and Naturalization Service (INS) until they could identify his actual parents.[2] Karjopranoto was convicted on April 25 by Thai authorities for using a fake passport. Both he and the Chinese woman were deported. As the investigation progressed, it was learned that the boy had been drugged. Furthermore, Got had been to Japan twice, and this was his second trip to Los Angeles. He was used as a decoy by an organized crime group to traffic women from Thailand and China to the United States and Japan: "Phanupong Khaisee, three, had been used at least twice to help a racket bring Asian women into the United States,"[3] a fact confirmed in another report: "The boy's passport showed two previous trips to Japan and one to the United States."[4]

After a telephone conversation with Ladawan Wongsriwong, President of the Young Northern Women's Development Foundation, regarding Got's case, I received a number of calls from a local NGO in Los Angeles. The staff member and Ladawan agreed that it would be in the best interest of the little boy for his paternal grandparents, Boonlue and Sumalee Khaisri, to visit him in Los Angeles. I was asked to help provide funds for airplane tickets for the grandparents. So with the help of my colleagues at Loma Linda University and members of the Thai Seventh-Day Adventist Church, enough money was raised to purchase one ticket, while the local NGO paid for the other. Pastor Somchai Piromgraipakd, senior pastor of the Thai Seventh-Day Adventist Church arranged for them to stay at White Memorial Hospital, Los Angeles. Their two-week accommodation plan turned into six months. At the request of Wongsriwong, I made many visits to the grandparents. It was during these visits that Tabtim became to me more than just a name in the newspaper. I started wondering about her life story, her history.

According to *The Washington Post,* May 15, 2000, human rights advocates are disturbed by the boy's family history, a history that seems to reflect a cycle of abuse. According to the Coalition to Abolish Slavery and Trafficking, the boy was born in Chiang Rai Province, a region known for sex trade trafficking. His mother was sold into sexual slavery at the age of twelve, and it is believed that she is a drug addict, unfit to be a mother, especially now that she lives with a trafficker. (His father committed suicide after learning that he was HIV positive.)[5]

THE CYCLE OF ABUSE

After listening to stories of her childhood life, her family, her journey to Chiang Mai and Bangkok, I asked what happened to Got. I was interested in her perception of the case.

After Wiwat passed away, Tabtim left Chiang Rai and headed for Bangkok. She asked her mother to take care of her son, Got.

According to one reporter, Tabtim "moved to Bangkok and married an ethnic Chinese man named Ma Chao Yong with Singaporean papers who, Thai authorities believe, is involved in trafficking human beings."[6]

In Bangkok, she met an Indonesian man, Suseno. They quickly became close friends. Suseno visited Got often and brought him candies and toys. The two, Tabtim observed, got along really well. One day, Suseno asked if he could take Got sightseeing. Noticing how well they got along, she agreed. By her own account, Tabtim did not realize that Suseno was part of a trafficking ring.

According to police sources, "Tubtim Kaewpaengchan, 22, told investigators she had let a friend look after her son and was unaware he had been taken to the US."[7] According to a reporter, her father said that, "she half jokingly told us then that she would sell the boy for 10,000 baht."[8]

"How did you come to hear the news about Got being detained by U.S. immigration?" I inquired.

She had received a call from a U.S. immigration officer asking her to identify herself and to fax her house registration, ID, and Got's passport to the U.S. consulate in Bangkok.

I recalled our initial conversation. "If you could tell the public about this case, what would you like to tell them?"

Tabtim stared at her drink. The quiet pause was not about searching for the right words. In a soft voice, she told me she wished to let them know that she never sold her son.

This statement does not sound very convincing to investigators and human rights groups. "Standing between them is an army of skeptics here and in the US who find it hard to believe the Thai mother unknowingly let a suspected Indonesian gangster take her boy out of the country to pose as the son of fake parents."[9]

Did Tabtim really sell her son to the trafficking ring? Perhaps we will never find out what truly happened. It is easier for the psyche to think in black and white—that right is right and wrong is wrong. People's lives, however, are a multicolored reality. Could it be that Tabtim knew something illegal was going on? It is easy to think that a good mother never sells her son and a bad mother will do anything for money. Life is more mysterious than either-or propositions, with more gray areas than we wish to acknowledge. Could it be possible for an unfit mother to love her son? When someone is driven into the arms of strangers for love and money at such a young age, could it be possible to rationalize one's actions so that the focus readjusts, and the difference between black and white becomes visibly gray? I do not think that Tabtim knew of the trafficking activity, although she might have suspected that something shady was going on. Perhaps she thought that her son would have a great time sight-seeing and she would also gain from his trip. However we view this case and her motives, a victim does exist. This young child is a victim of dichotomized thinking, that there is no wrong in right nor right in wrong because all is black or white.

People do not like to perceive themselves as bad, and if they do bad things, they often believe they have good reasons. Soi Pradu is a narrow lane in the middle of Rayong City. It was through Pa Klae, a brothel owner, that this lane became known for sex. The Soi Pradu brothel was known for its atrocities; it was Pa Klae's tradition to rape all the girls before sending them out to entertain clients. He hired pimps to beat them with pipes to keep them under control. It was reported that 80 percent of his prostitutes are HIV positive. During the police investigation, Pa Klae admitted that, given a chance, he would continue his business because the government is not doing anything to help these girls. He is the one helping them by giving them jobs and improving their economic status. Beating them is only an attempt to prevent them from escaping, a punishment.[10] Rationalization seems necessary to maintain one's sense of self.

We do not really know what happened between Tabtim and her son, but the one thing I do know is that she does not want people to think of her as a bad person who is willing to sell even her own son. Still, Got is now in Los Angeles, a victim of human trafficking.

TRAFFICKING

According to the United Nations, international victims of trafficking number approximately 200 million, and trafficking is one of the fastest growing criminal enterprises.[11] According to the United Nations, trafficking in women refers to

[a]ll acts involved in the recruitment and/or transportation of a woman (or a girl) within and across national borders for work or service by means of violence, abuse of authority or dominant position, debt bondage, deception or other forms of coercion.[12]

It is estimated that approximately 1.5 million people migrate into and out of Thailand. This amounts to 5 percent of the total labor force of 32 million Thais. Remittances from the out-bound labor force in 1995, according to a report by the Bank of Thailand, are estimated at 45,700 million baht, whereas in 1976 remittances totaled only 485 million baht. In 1994, remittances accounted for 15 percent of the trade deficits.[13] According to Pasuk Phongpaichit, Sungsidh Piryarangsan, and Nualnoi Treerat, professors of economics at Chulalongkorn University, "Illegal trafficking in labour arises because governments refuse to recognize the economic need for imported manual labour. Imperfect information about job availability, access, and mobility make these potential migrants prey to agents and labour recruiters."[14]

Although the number of sex workers being trafficked into other countries is not known, it is known that the amount of money generated from organized criminal syndicates is substantial. Wanchai Roujanavong, Senior Expert State Attorney, Office of the Attorney General, estimates the total at 45 to 54 billion baht, making this the most profitable in comparison to all illegal businesses.[15] Here is where the cycle begins: more money equals more power; more power means more influence over corrupt officials who will help to expand their territory so they can traffic more women into the sex industry; more women means more money, and the cycle continues. In Roujanavong's observation, the severity of laws does not prevent traffickers from using influence, bribes, or violence to escape punishment.[16]

OUTBOUND

Although some women were lured into the sex trade, a number give consent to be trafficked for financial reasons. Those who do sign a contract agreeing to pay the inflated cost of the loan set by the traffickers. A typical deal is to sleep with 400 to 500 clients to cover the money borrowed. Such agreements are often made in total ignorance of the fact that they will be detained in brothels against their will and forfeit their passports to the traffickers. Without passports, freedom to move around, and communication skills, these women become vulnerable slaves, easy prey for those waiting to take advantage of them. The benefit the traffickers earn is ten times the women's cost. One woman testified in court that she had to sleep with 400 clients in three months. If she could not attract 400 clients in three months, the number increased to 500 clients. A forty-five-minute service is priced at US$130, of which the trafficker receives $100, and the brothel owner, $30. This means a trafficker earns $40,000 in three months (or $50,000 in four months).[17]

Japan

Between 1991 and 1994, 20,982 Thai females were deported from Japan as illegal workers. Many had no proper travel documents as they had entered Japan using fake passports of other nationalities. About 80 percent had worked in sex services. Agents who helped them to enter Japan charged them a fee of around eight hundred thousand baht per person and then made them provide sex to clients to pay off this "debt." Agents had made an estimated net gain of over four billion baht a year from trafficking these women.[18]

Trafficking of Southeast Asian women to Japan on a large scale started around the 1970s and 1980s when NGOs and feminist movements in Japan and the Philippines protested against sex tourism by Japanese men. In the 1980s, when Prime Minister Aquino started her campaign against traffickers by policing the international airport, many corrupt officials were charged with cooperation with traffickers. This made it difficult for traffickers to traffic women out of the Philippines and into Japan. Thailand became their next target, and the 1980s saw a rapid growth in trafficking women to Japan for sex services that peaked in the early 1990s. A former Thai consul in Japan reported the number of 23,000 Thai sex workers in 1995, based on the number of Thai workers overstaying their visas. The actual number would be higher, since many others entered using fake non-Thai passports.[19]

Trafficking of Thai women to Japan is done through collaborative efforts by Japanese and Thai agents who provide passports, visas, airplane tickets, and basic Japanese language instruction. The *Daily News,* July 12, 1997, reported the arrest of a Japanese gang leader in Thailand who attempted to smuggle forty women into Japan in suitcases.[20] It takes, on average, nine to twelve months for a woman to pay back her debt through prostitution. In 1995 it was estimated that a Thai prostitute generated an annual income of 1.5 million baht. Of this amount, 25 percent went to the Thai agents and 75 percent to the mama-san who charged the woman for her debt, food, and lodging. After paying off her debt, the prostitute can operate as a freelance worker, but often prostitutes get arrested after spending a year in Japan, and this timing may not be accidental, since mama-sans earn more from bonded sex workers.[21]

Roujanavong recalls a story of a Thai woman lured and trafficked into Japan by a Yakusas gang. She was promised legitimate employment with good remuneration. Upon arrival she was kept as a sex object by the gang after serving as a prostitute for some time. After several years of violence and abuse, a gang member took interest in her but was murdered right in front of her. She fled. She was sought after by the Japanese prosecutor as a witness against the group, but fear kept her from testifying. She lives in fear today.[22]

Germany

Germany is the largest European market for Thai prostitutes. Out of the 6,000 prostitutes in Germany, according to one NGO's estimate, approximately 2,000 are Thais. In Germany prostitution is legal, but foreigners cannot work without a permit. Sex workers enter Germany using tourist visas. They can either choose to arrange their own visas and airplane tickets (40,000 baht) or have agents arrange travel for them (the price ranges from 140,000 to 560,000 baht).

Whereas an average German freelance prostitute in a big city earns 2,000 marks per day, a Thai prostitute under the control of a pimp retains only 2.5 percent of her total income, so that a day's work provides her with only 150 to 200 marks.[23]

Dara was born in Korat, a northeastern province of Thailand. After completing sixth grade, Dara started working as a servant for a German couple who came to her village to build a water reservoir. At the age of sixteen they invited her to work for them in Germany. Upon arrival they took away her passport. She was kept as a slave, working long hours. In addition to having to clean, she was also forced to have sex with the male owner. When he left for a job in Africa, his wife sold Dara to a bar owner. At the bar, the owner arranged for her to marry a German so she could obtain a permit to stay. She and her husband became addicted to drugs. After they both managed to rid themselves of drugs, they went to Thailand. But home was no longer a home for her, when she was constantly being condemned for the life that had been forced upon her. The glorious future of life in a European country turned out to be a nightmare that her family and society could not embrace. She returned to Germany with her husband, as a procurer of prostitutes, bringing with her other girls from the red-light district of Patpong in downtown Bangkok.[24]

United States

Michael Rostoker, a Silicon Valley executive, was charged by federal prosecutors for negotiating to buy a thirteen-year-old Vietnamese girl, Dung, from her family and bring her to the United States for sex. During the month of April he went to Vietnam with the intention of forging Dung's birth certificate to show that she was eighteen so that he could marry her and bring her back to the United States as his wife. The numerous e-mail messages that he exchanged with Dung contained his advice for her to stay slim and pretty in order to satisfy his sexual desire. When Dung wrote back stating that she was too young for sex, Rostoker scolded her: "In Saigon, it is easy to find girls who are 12+ years of age (younger than you) who are prostitutes for sex," he wrote in the e-mail, "so AGE is NOT an excuse."[25]

Theresa Boar, head of the State Department's Office for Internaional Women's Issues, believes that "[a]s many as 50,000 women and children are brought to the United States each year to be forced into prostitution, bonded sweatshop labor and domestic servitude."[26] Underground brothels with foreign sex workers exist in big cities such as New York, Los Angeles, Seattle, and San Diego. They are typically located in Chinatown areas operated by Asian gangs. Women from Thailand being trafficked into the United States are sold by Thai agents to local mama-sans for $18,000 to $43,000. The mama-sans usually make three times the amount they pay. A mama-san who turned state witness admitted that most mama-sans "have no intention of setting the women free until they are no longer usable."[27] A prostitute is forced to entertain 200 to 400 customers in order to cover the purchase debt incurred by the mama-san. She is also charged $1,200 per month for room and board, and this means entertaining an extra twelve customers per month. She receives nothing but tips from customers and is confined to the establishment. The annual income per victim of the sex trade is approximately 1.9 million baht, with

150,000 to 375,000 baht paid to the Thai agent and the remaining to the mama-san.[28]

Kathryn McMahon, Director of Research, Coalition to Abolish Slavery and Trafficking, recalls the case of a young Chinese woman abducted from her village in China and taken by boat to Mexico and then by plane to New York:

> While in New York, she was beaten, raped and tattooed with the insignia of the gang, which claimed to own her. Then she was taken to Los Angeles where she was forced to work in various brothels for six years. At one point she managed to escape but did not speak any English and did not know where to go for help. She was apprehended by her traffickers, beaten on the street, dragged into a car and taken back to the brothel. She escaped a second time and found a Chinese grocery store where employees could understand her pleas for help and called police.[29]

INBOUND

With various government and NGO campaigns combating child prostitution in Thailand, traffickers turned to recruiting foreign children as substitutes. Research by Kritaya Archavanitkul and Pornsuk Kerdsawang of Mahidol University, surveying forty commercial sex businesses during 1996, did not find new Thai girls from northern Thailand entering the sex business for the past three years. They found instead many foreign girls being recruited from the Mekong subregion, from places such as Burma, Laos, and China. Women from Shan State in China and other minority groups from the northwestern (Thai-Burmese) border were the largest groups represented. Poverty and the lack of employment were the main factors that pushed these women to seek better-paying jobs in Thailand. They mostly used the service of traffickers who, through influence, were able to negotiate with officials at the Chinese-Myanmar and Myanmar-Thai borders.[30] Although many consented they did not realize the types of abuse and coercion they had to face while in the hands of traffickers. If they were to change their minds they would be threatened by violence or starved until they decided to obey.

Burma/Myanmar

Sometime in 1993, while working for the Adventist Development and Relief Agency in Bangkok, I received a letter from a Burmese activist describing the situation of a brothel in the south,
complete with pictures of the inside of the brothel with its small cubicles. The activist, Yin Htwe, after reporting the atrocity of the
Ranong brothel to the CPCR, fled for his life and was granted political asylum in the United States. July 14, 1993, the police raided the
Vida, Victoria, and Sonthaya brothels run by Pinai Nakaew, a former police corporal. The commandos forced their way into the
brothels and found many young girls aged fifteen to twenty in tiny
cubicles where they were forced to prostitute themselves.[31] Ob-
serving the condition of the brothel, Theerapol Veerawat of CPCR
stated, "The stench of the place was terrible. There were no proper
toilets. It was a hell hole."[32]

As a result of this raid, 144 Burmese women and nine pimps were
arrested. Of the 144 women, forty were under the age of eighteen and
several of them were pregnant. Forty-three of them tested HIV positive. They were all locked into one cell, which was so crowded that
they had to take turns lying down. On September 15, 1993, ninety-
five of them were repatriated. Anna was not among the ninety-five;
she was sent to a rehabilitation home. The tragic story of her life was
told by Ron O'Grady of ECPAT.

Anna was born into a Karen tribe that lived along the Thai-
Burmese border. Her tribe was under constant threat from the Burmese government. At the age of fourteen Anna woke one early morning to the sound of gunfire. She soon learned that the nearby village
was surrounded by the Burmese military force. After cruel interroga-
tions meant to solicit confessions of terrorism, the Karen men were
forced to dig a large pit. They were shot and buried in the pit that they
had been forced to dig. Women and children were locked in a build-
ing where men could freely enter to rape them.

Anna's family decided that she should escape to the border and
stay at the refugee camp. She and two other friends left for the border.
Tears and the embrace from her parents were her last memory of her
family. At the camp she soon learned that her future depended on
her willingness to take greater risks. She headed for Bangkok and
was most unfortunate to be caught without any form of identification

or permission. Anna was returned to the Burmese border, where she was raped by the guards. A couple of days later a Burmese woman paid her bail and Anna was released. This woman was a procurer for the sex trade. On her fifteenth birthday Anna arrived at a brothel in Ranong, a town with 100,000 Burmese seamen with 300 Burmese fishing boats at the port daily. Her customers beat her, and when she reported to the guards, she was again beaten for being ungrateful. She soon became pregnant but was still required to see the same number of customers. When she reported to the pimps that the pain was unbearable, they induced miscarriage by beating her in the stomach until she bled and fainted. Her friends collected enough money from tips to send her to the hospital. She was saved, but not her child.[33]

Describing the situation of Burmese sex workers in Thailand Phongpaichit, Piriyarangsan, and Treerat of Chulalongkorn University, state, "As brothels become more concealed, women become more exploited. The protection fees paid to the police increase and the women are made to work harder to defray this cost."[34] The level of concealment creates another problem:

> As they are illegal immigrants working in an illegal trade, Burmese prostitutes often work in underground brothels. They service low-paid males and have to provide many services a day. In such third and fourth-rate places, it is very easy to contract sexually-transmitted diseases and AIDS. Police raids on brothels with young (under eighteen) Burmese and hill women in the mid 1990s revealed a high incidence of HIV-positive [women rescued from brothels] (up to 40 percent).[35]

China

During my many visits with Got's grandparents discussing his case, the legal matters, and Tabtim's life, I learned from Boonlue Khaisri that many Chinese girls from Xishuangbanna, Yunnan, work as commercial sex workers in Thailand. Vorasakdi Mahatdhanobol, researcher at the Asian Research Center for Migration, Institute of Asian Studies, Chulalongkorn University, believes that approximately 500 to 1,500 Chinese women are trafficked into Thailand as commercial sex workers. This estimate is based on the report by a Chinese official that, in 1991, 3,000 women went missing from Yunnan.[36] Most Chinese women trafficked into Thailand are from Yunnan Province, located on the southwestern part of China, sharing its border, which extends for 4,060 kilometers, with Laos, Burma, and Vietnam. The net income from Chinese women trafficked into Thailand's sex trade is approximately 10 million to 30 million baht.[37]

Stories of hope and tragedy of these Chinese women have been documented by Mahatdhanobol based on his interviews with thirty-five victims of trafficking from Yunnan. In 1991, police helped five Chinese women who escaped from a brothel in Bangkok and placed them under the care of the CPCR. This brought to light the presence of Chinese women in the Thai sex trade. Mahatdhanobol made a number of trips to Yunnan to interview Chinese women rescued from the sex trade, to offer their accounts of how they were deceived. The reasons these women became vulnerable to trafficking involved the new economic policy initiated by Deng Xiaoping in 1979, argued Mahatdhanobol:

> The wishes of the 35 women for better lives would not have arisen so strongly if the Chinese government had used development policies like those of Mao Zedong's era. During that time, the government did not support the population's attempt to find security and happiness in the manner of capitalist countries. People could not choose the jobs they desired of those with high pay. They were not able to travel freely to cities and see the progress there. But present policies are not those of Mao's era and the continuous flow of information into rural areas has affected ideas about consumption. Being modern and wealthy in a western style is a kind of new basis for consumption. The new forms of information available to rural people naturally charm them.[38]

Deception

Most of the thirty-five women were approached by acquaintances or by agents themselves, inviting the girls to go sight-seeing at the Burmese or Thai border. Some were invited to work in Thailand or Burma for higher-paying jobs. The average age of these girls was eighteen. They were young and wanted to see the world as advertised through television and radio, the charm of big-city life. Most of them did not inform their parents before leaving, since it was supposedly just a day trip. For those who intended to go to work, the plan was to get a job and then write home. They figured that bringing lots of money back to the family would at least justify their actions. One of the girls was lured by a group of men riding in a pickup truck taxi. They asked her to get into the truck and travel with them for two hours. By the time she learned her actual situation, it was too late. According to the report, "she was not suspicious of them, explaining that until her encounter with the pickup truck, she had never been lied to or deluded to such an extent."[39]

The Routes

Geographical landscape and type of deception determine the mode of transportation. Girls who were told that jobs waited for them at the border or in Burma often crossed at Jinghong. Some women traveled by motorized vehicles all the way to Kengtung, a city in Burma, since the roads are well paved. Women from Lancang County, due to the geographical terrain and the distance, often traveled by motorized vehicle to the border and then walked the rest of the way. Those who walked often realized as they maneuvered through difficult terrain that something was not right. Their reaction was met with intimidation, guns and knives, beating and starving. Seven of the thirty-five women who walked for twenty days through the forest until they reached the Thai border often slept by the roadside. Along the way, the women were transferred to the responsibility of another group, yet during this period none of the girls suspected that they were destined to work as commercial sex workers. The possibility occurred to them only after they had crossed the border at Mae Sai, Chiang Rai. They knew then that they would be sold, and resisting such an attempt meant going without food and shelter. Once they crossed the border, they were sent to various provinces, such as Chiang Rai (north); Bangkok (central); Narathiwat, Songkla, and Yala (south). These women were told that they had to repay expenses incurred but never knew how much they had to earn. The understanding was that they would have to work for at least one year. They received nothing for their services except accommodation and food.

Commercial Sex Workers

Upon learning of their predicament, the unavoidable sex services, none could accept. They all shared one common factor: they had hope—they were hoping to escape from the establishment. When their attempts failed and their services became more frequent, hope faded. A new feeling overcame them: *fah likit,* literally translated as destiny. Its Chinese equivalent is *tien-ming:* heaven determines our destiny. Once the chart is set, the course has to be followed. For two of the women, the commercial sex was good business; they earned income that would not have been possible for them in Yunnan:

> The feelings of these two women demonstrate how their desires changed between the time of their initial incarceration to the time of their release. They said that after learning they had been deceived into the sex trade, they both wished to escape. However, after a long period of selling sex, they became convinced that life in the brothel was their fah likit.[40]

THE FUTURE

Reflecting on future trends, Mahatdhanobol is of the opinion that this economic progress will most likely result in more girls entering the commercial sex scene of their own will for economic growth and survival. It is no longer dim hope leading to *fah likit; fah likit* has now become their hope. Sex is no longer that which they seek to escape; it has become their escape route from poverty.

Noi, a fourteen-year-old Burmese girl whose parents struggle in the fields to cover medical expenses for her younger brother, wrote:

> She [the Madam] told me that I could do this work if I wanted to or I could do any other work that I wanted. However, if I did this work I would quickly earn more money. I went to her house [the Madam was from the same village as Noi], which is in Chiang Tung [Shan State, Myanmar]. I told her that I wanted to work, I had no money, and I wanted to help my parents. She told me "please don't worry I will help you, you don't have to cry. I will go back to Thailand now but I will send someone to pick you up." And she did send someone to pick me up. I went with two friends, when we reached Mae Sai she met us.[41]

Mahatdhanobol's analysis of the impact of the transition from Mao Zedong's policies to Deng Xiaoping's on young women confirms Khao-Ngam's concern:

Despise material progress
And economic prosperity,
Still too much strain and stress
Cause our children injury.[42]

Finally, asked Khao-Ngam, "If a child reminds sad, how bad our future must be?"[43]

Chapter 8

Reflection

Where are you, my dreamer, tonight?
Go heighten your consciousness,
Then add colours, sound and light,
O'er the real image of hideousness.

So Humans can regain our dignity
And honours that none should shame;
Tho' a dreamer may derive no pity,
He's ready to die lighting life's flame.

Paiwarin Khao-Ngam
"The Flame and the Dreamer"

I am a child of the baby boom era born into ideology, inspired to fight the unbeatable foe and run where the brave dare not go, figuratively. Life's meaning lies in that task of restoring dignity to humanity and perhaps being ready to die "lighting life's flame." Not that I am interested in dying, but I gravitate toward the romance of such an ideology. Child prostitution seemed the right battle to pick, yet somehow that romantic ideology slowly faded through my conversations with Tabtim and others in similar circumstances. The final lesson learned is one of introspection. The seed of greed lies within, and one is left with a very special journey into the depth of one's very own spirituality. Perhaps this journey is not so much that of dying to light life's flame but lighting the flame so that we may recognize urges, needs, wants, and longings within us. This light dawned on me through my conversations with the Rahabs and the Mary Magdalenes. God speaks using radical instruments to address the issues that lie at the core of our lives. In listening I hope to find insights into my soul.

After completing his chant at a funeral house in Anaheim, a Laotian Buddhist monk waited for his ride while smoking his cigarette. I approached him with the question "What is the purpose of chanting?"

"It is to remind the dead that she is dead."

"If she is dead, why do we have to remind her that she is dead?

"Because she does not know that she is dead."

I pondered the concept of reincarnation. Perhaps it makes sense in his worldview.

"Where does she go after her death?"

"The spirit roams around for a couple of days."

"Why?"

"Because it takes time for the gatekeeper of Hades to figure out where she is going to go. He has to check her records and tally her good and bad deeds. It takes time to go through the whole book."

Although I do not share his worldview, belief in the cycle of reincarnation, I cannot help but wonder about the judgment the gatekeeper of Hades would pronounce on Jan, a prostitute who died of AIDS at the age of nineteen. The monks would need to chant longer in Jan's case, since the body in the coffin would be a stranger to Jan herself. Tallying Jan's good and bad deeds, what would be her cumulative? The balance? Would she be in the red?

Jan wanted to dress pretty and send home money. Nong wanted to support her two children through school. Nid wanted to start a small shop selling clothes. Nari wanted to relieve her parents' heavy responsibilities. Jinda wanted to be a singer. Tabtim wanted to leave her conflicted home environment.

Flipping my notepad to the page before last, I asked Tabtim what she enjoyed doing.

"Cleaning house," she said. I thought that was a good answer. But there was one other thing. "I like to go see a fortune teller."

"What did the fortune teller tell you?"

"He said my star speaks favorably of me and advised me to start a restaurant. He also told me that my life partner would be rich, fair, and older."

I noticed a very hopeful smile on her face.

If there were a gatekeeper of Hades, what would he have written in her book? She wants a life partner who is rich, fair, and older. Would it take long to tally her deeds and decide her destiny? When I was young, I used to watch a Thai TV program about a gatekeeper of

Hades by the name Suwan. Somehow I can't help but wonder if we are all Suwans, recording notes in our books, judging human destiny? We create heaven or hell through our judgment, our discourse. We shape and form human identity through categories that we as a society determine.

When the Aryans, the warrior race, moved to north India and subjugated the Dravidians, the natives, they dictated the norms and spelled out the caste system. They constructed a hierarchy and decided who were the untouchables. Of course they were not the untouchables. He who has the power decides the place for others. These constructed norms have impacted millions of lives and are used to defined social relations, the formation of one's identity. Those with power dictate norms and form others' identities.

This pattern repeats itself in other areas of life. Is it possible that we proliferate mental illness when we create more diagnostic criteria and categories of psychopathology? Social constructions have such power to dictate how we feel and how we perceive ourselves, as if the interplay between our genetic predisposition and social constructions dictates who we are. By internalizing this, we take part in defining others through the given norms. The power of norms is such that we have to live by them, deny them, or rationalize our behavior as good.

The glitter of desirable objects flashing on TV screens constantly redefines norms and constructs the criteria of a good life. Advertising agencies have so convincingly persuaded us that wants are needs, we come to believe we cannot live without certain things. The wooden house with a thatch roof, which was once normative, has now become undesirable. Those buffalo pulling plows in the fields are now symbols of poverty; a machine is the preferred tool. More objects flashing on TV screens and we feel poorer and poorer. Could it be that poverty is first conceived in the minds of those in marketing? Perhaps we are socially constructed to feel, perceive, and judge in a certain way, and any movement we make is from one social group to another. Listening to the stories of the Rahabs and Mary Magdalenes disturbs me deeply because the clear distinct line between them and me is gradually fading. It disturbs me because it is easier to patronize, so that I can feel good about myself, but when the line fades, I begin to see my face reflected in their eyes.

Jan was fourteen and her poverty was partly real and partly constructed. The posters, shops, and television forced a reassessment of her life. Her friends returning from the south wore pretty dresses and makeup, and, thus, conceptually, her level of poverty intensified. She went south, thereby writing her own obituary. Suwan, flipping through his short book of records, tallied her deeds quickly and thought, "She is not going to make it through the gates." I am beginning to realize that my categories, as well as constructed norms, determined Jan's identity. I saw Jan as a prostitute dying of AIDS. I did not see a daughter, a sister, a friend. Negotiating sex was only a part of her life. It is sad that this portion of her life dictated the formation of her total identity. Jan was socialized to experience the intensity of her poverty, to feel the emptiness of her life. Without sufficient social support, she picked an escape route that sealed her destiny. Through the mass media she was told what she should attain. Through whisperings of friends and neighbors, she was told that she could not attain this except through selling her body.

We all have needs and wants. Some have more means to attain those wants and needs, while some have very limited means. We strive to be worth something, to attain status or possessions. Our needs and wants are often determined by our community, which defines success and failure, good and bad. We live by these norms, and through this socialization process we form our identity—and we keep striving.

What have I learned from listening? As people with needs and wants, we have moments of greed and generosity. In wanting to be worth something, often the striving never ceases. It only takes different forms—some more acceptable and some less dignifying than others.

The changing forms of the sex trade in Thailand suggest the tragedy of human souls trapped in the socialization process. They stand as testimony to the striving urge perpetuated by a growing economy. Campaign after campaign has been launched against child prostitution and the sex industry. New bills have been implemented, and new systems constructed. Projects focusing on the prevention of child prostitution have mushroomed in various parts of the country. Many of these programs have achieved a high level of success in their targeted populations, yet we face multiple forms of the sex industry. There has been a massive reduction in the number of brothels, but an increase in cocktail lounges, karaoke bars, cafés, and massage parlors. Despite new laws and projects, basic human urges remain. Buddha was right when he named mankind's greatest tragedy as desire, or *tanha*.[1]

The sex industry is a symptom of a bigger problem we all have to face: wants that have been intensified through social constructions, wants that lead us in search of ourselves through wealth, power, status, honor, recognition, and appreciation. And because we can never find ourselves this way, urges remain, and striving never ceases. Pimps want more power, agents more wealth, prostitutes more income, and men more sex. Desire does not cease because it deceptively leads us further away from ourselves. The proliferation of the sex industry is an invitation to us to listen carefully. We certainly wish to resolve this problem, but the problem becomes a voice urging us to listen to its meaning, to look deeper into ourselves, because all actions have a ripple effect. Wants will always remain, and pursuing them will not help us attain our sense of self. Pursuing is an illusion that leads us further from ourselves. Returning to ourselves is to find rest in the midst of our limitations. Krisnamurti states:

> As long as one is a slave to society, as long as one is greedy, envious, ambitious, pursuing pleasure, prestige, seeking status through function—as long as one is not free of all that, there can be no renewal, no freshness, no rejuvenation, no silence, no freedom.[2]

"Blessed are the poor in spirit," said Jesus, "for theirs is the kingdom of heaven."

Listening to Rahab has taught me that we are all alike in many ways. The difference is, some have more means than others. We are socialized to want things a certain way, and in pursuing that, we are further alienated, widening the gap between these children and us, increasing their level of poverty and intensifying their desire. Returning disengages us from this cycle. The challenge is to find the courage to embrace ourselves in the midst of societal pressure to attain or achieve a predefined definition of being. The challenge is to take those steps in the path of self-definition because every self-differentiated step we make may indirectly deter an adolescent girl from entering the trade that seals her destiny. Every such step that we take weakens the power of social constructions and hence reduces the power of wants that so strongly motivates agents and pimps. Every self-differentiated step we take offers young girls the courage to choose self-dignity. Every act of sharing increases means and opportunities, providing alternatives, and narrows the gap between us and them, increasing their comfort level with who they are.

I have a dream. My dream is not to strip these children of wants and desire but to help them rediscover a new passion, for self-appreciation that transcends societal expectations fueled by consumerism. The task seems enormous, but I find comfort in knowing "a frog can dream once in a while."

Afterword

I have often been asked what Thailand has done to deal with this problem of child prostitution. I wish to end this book by affirming the tremendous amount of effort invested by local NGOs and government agencies in dealing with this issue. On the day Busarin Wareesangtip, Warren Scale, and I went to visit Ladawan Wongsriwong, Deputy Minister of Labor and Social Welfare, the first thing we were introduced to was a draft of a new bill addressing the current situation of the sex industry in Thailand, that is, the proliferation of sexual services concealed behind various forms of entertainment. This illustrates the deliberate efforts on the part of the Thai government to deal with this issue. Since first meeting Ladawan Wongsriwong, I have been deeply inspired by her dedication to help deter children from entering the sex trade; the risks she takes facing local influential individuals involved in the sex trade in Phayao Province; her support of the Prevention and Suppression of Prostitution Act of 1996; her educational programs for poor children; her attempts to foster in women and children the need to cultivate and maintain their dignity and self-respect. She is just one of many others who have dedicated their lives to the future of poor children in Thailand. The following paragraph, taken from an ECPAT report, illustrates the efforts to combat the problem of child prostitution in Thailand:

> In Thailand, there are indications that there has been a substantial reduction in the number of children in prostitution in Northern Thailand. There is an increasing awareness of child prostitution and AIDS amongst school children and the number of children remaining in school in the region has increased considerably. In the district of Chiang Rai, only 49% of children who had finished primary school in 1990 started the first year of secondary school. In comparison, by 1999 this figure had reached 90%. This indicates that the measures that the Thai government and NGO's have been taking to prevent commercial sexual exploitation of children are having a positive impact. These measures include the provision of scholarships to girls at risk to allow them to remain in school under

the Sema Life Development Programme. Schoolteachers have also been mobilized in an effort to prevent children from being lured into prostitution. The Department of Public Welfare has established seven vocational training centers which provide vocational training to disadvantaged young women. . . . Following the vocational courses, assistance is given to help participants get a job and soft loans are provided to help the participants set up income-generating activities. Overall it seems apparent that there has been a decline in child prostitution in recent years due to economic development, increases in educational opportunities, awareness about HIV/AIDS, access to information, and government and NGO initiatives.[1]

All these efforts through legislation, education, prevention, rehabilitation, and vocation need to continue because they relieve pain and provide safety for countless children in Thailand. We are also faced with new challenges, and in reflecting on these, I wish only to suggest that introspection be added into this whole process. The courage to take a self-differentiated step in the midst of our strengths and infirmities may be the final challenge we have to face before we can provide genuine affirmation to these children.

Appendix

Global Incidence of Child Prostitution

North Africa

Information on child prostitution in this area is very limited. Few governments admit that the problem of child prostitution exists, except in Egypt and Algeria. One official estimates 168 cases in Egypt between 1995 and 1996. The most visible types of sex trade are child sex tourism and prostitution by street children. Child sex tourism takes place mostly in Morocco and Egypt.

West Africa

As in North Africa, statistics and information are lacking due to insufficient awareness of the issue. Information received indicates that the problem exists and is related to poverty, high rates of urbanization, lack of education, and insufficient alternative means for survival. In some countries, war is the main contributing factor. In Sierra Leone and Liberia, where civil war has been raging for the past nine years and a large majority of the population has been displaced, prostitution among teenage girls is increasing. There are reports of children being abducted by rebels and used as sex slaves. In Liberia, some girls are being contracted as spouses for expatriates and Liberians abroad.

This appendix is based mainly on the compilation of information by ECPAT International in *Looking Back, Thinking Forward: A Fourth Report on the Implementation of the Agenda for Action Adopted at the First World Congress Against Commercial Sexual Exploitation of Children in Stockholm, Sweden, 28 August 1996,* and on information provided in other compilations by ECPAT. Some figures may differ, but this is due to different sources of information gathered through diverse methodologies.

Central and East Africa

In Ethiopia, child prostitution is widespread in urban areas, especially in Addis Ababa, due to poverty, unemployment, migration, and family breakdown. It is not uncommon to see children between thirteen and fifteen roaming the streets in Addis Ababa after 7:00 p.m. looking for clients. In Kenya sex tourism is prevalent. Girls in this trade number approximately 10,000 to 30,000. Tour guides often take tourists to locations where girls can be found. According to one report, as many as 40,000 children live on the streets and many of them survive through prostitution. In Uganda, the Lord's Resistance Army abducted 10,000 boys and girls in the past two years. Some of these girls were forced to marry their captors. A total of 800 children are in prostitution in some areas of Tanzania. In February 2000, police raided a local evangelical church in Burundi and discovered forty people working as prostitutes.

Southern Africa

Among southern African countries, child prostitution exists in various forms and mostly occurs in South Africa and Zambia. The Child Welfare Movement reported 431 cases of child prostitution in 1998 to 1999. Some of these girls may be as young as eight or ten years old. One common phenomenon of child sexual abuse is that of "sugar daddies," older men who provide school fees, food, clothes, and gifts for young girls in exchange for sex.

North and Central America

Increased sexual exploitation in North and Central America is attributed to a number of factors, such as poverty, sexual abuse, increasing rural-to-urban migration and family disintegration. The highest rate of child sex tourism is in Costa Rica, and it is related to the fact that Asian countries and the United States have toughened their controls on child sex tourism, whereas information on sex tourism in Costa Rica is readily available. San José is regarded as the center of sex tourism for Costa Rica and Central America. The strengthening of the laws in the United States has also driven pedophiles toward these regions. In Mexico, particularly Guadalajara, victims of child sex tourism are often boys. In El Salvador, 30 to 35 percent of prostitutes are girls under the age of eighteen.

In the United States at least 100,000 children are believed to be involved in commercial sexual exploitation. According to UNICEF, State of the World's Children, 1997, 300,000 to 600,000 juveniles are involved in prostitution in the United States. It is believed that each year between 1.2 million and 2 million teenagers hit the streets; half of these teenagers will turn to prostitution to survive.[1]

South America

There are six different forms of child prostitution in South America. The first form is that of street children whose clientele usually includes those in the lower socioeconomic level. These children work as prostitutes in order to survive. The second form refers to sexual exploitation in entertainment places, such as bars, massage parlors, and discotheques. The third form of sex industry is hidden and is carried out in private homes. This form is most prominent in Bolivia and Uruguay, and the perpetrators are associated with pedophile rings and are protected by people in power. The fourth form is something that is just starting to emerge. This form refers to schoolgirls or teenagers who prostitute themselves for financial reasons. The fifth form takes place mostly in areas where industries employ mainly males. The last form is that of sex tourism, and it is increasing in various parts of South America.

"In Brazil an estimated 1 million children are believed to enter the multi-billion dollar sex market each year."[2] One local NGO estimates that between 500,000 and 2 million children are forced into prostitution annually.[3]

Middle East

Although information on this issue is scarce in this region, there are many reported accounts of Middle Eastern nationals engaging in sex tourism, and most of these men are from Saudi Arabia, the United Arab Emirates, and Kuwait. Destinations often include Thailand, India, Pakistan, Morocco, Egypt, and Europe. Some accounts describe wealthy Saudi men traveling to these regions to offer a couple thousand dollars for native daughters. After a period, these men often leave these young girls and return to their own country.

South Asia

In India, "[p]rostitution is widespread, with an estimated 2.3 million prostitutes in the country, some 575,000 of whom are children."[4] The problem of child prostitution takes different forms in India, depending on the region. In major cities such as Bombay, Delhi, and Madras, many young girls are being trafficked from neighboring countries such as Nepal and Bangladesh. In Goa, a beach resort area, sex tourism is prevalent. The Devadasi system, in which young girls are sold to the temple and later turn to prostitution, is common in Karnataka, Maharashtra, and Andhra Pradesh. Some reports discuss young girls prostituting to supplement their income. In Sri Lanka, "beach boys" are found in various designated tourist areas. It is estimated that approximately 15,000 to 30,000 children are victims of sex tourism. In Pakistan there are reports of Arab men coming to buy children for short-term marriages. A system similar to that of Devadasi also exists in Nepal. According to UNICEF, 10,000 children are in prostitution in Bangladesh. Other estimates push that number to 29,000. According to Tabibul Islam, "Over the last decade, 200,000 Bangladeshi girls were lured under false circumstances and sold into the sex industry in nations including Pakistan, India and the Middle East."[5] It is estimated that twenty-five to fifty girls are trafficked out of Bangladesh for prostitution every month.[6]

East Asia

Throughout East Asian countries young girls enter prostitution both voluntarily and involuntarily. Those who volunteer do it for financial reasons or to supplement their income. Those forced into the sex industry are often trafficked into other countries or sold by their parents. According to UNICEF, "[o]ne third of 55,000 prostitutes in Cambodia are under 18 and most of them are Vietnamese."[7] In Cambodia, a family can earn $150 from selling their virgin daughter. Girls who are brought to Phnom Penh are almost always virgins. According to Madeline Eisner, "[c]hild prostitution flourishes in Cambodia with an estimated 20,000 girls and boys forced into the sex industry in that country alone."[8] Human Rights Vigilance of Cambodia, in 1995, reported that young girls ages twelve to seventeen comprised nearly 31 percent of prostitutes in Phnom Penh and eleven other provinces.[9] In Laos, where beer is sold, a child is required to sit by the adult. This method often leads to prostitution. *Enjo-kousai,* which literally translated means "to associate and keep company," is practiced in Japan, Korea, and Taiwan. This refers to schoolgirls offering companionship to their clients that may lead to sexual services. *Terekura,* telephone chat, is another type of sex service that is being practiced in Japan and the Republic of Korea. Through the phone conversation, a meeting place and time are arranged for sexual services.

Aphaluck Bhatiasevi reported that "[t]he number of Burmese women and girls traveling to Thailand through Mae Sai to enter the sex industry is increasing. 60 percent of them are under eighteen years of age."[10] ECPAT estimates 50,000 Burmese girls and women working in the Thai sex industry at any one time.[11]

> In Thailand the number of child prostitutes varies, 15,000 according to Ministry of Public Health, 30,000 according to Thai Red Cross and

200,000 according to ECPAT. The latter figures include girls brought to Thailand from countries such as Burma and Vietnam. [12]

Child prostitution in East Asian countries often takes place in bars, coffee shops, massage parlors, beauty salons, dance bars, karaoke bars, and brothels. These locations are more concealed in China and Vietnam.

Western Europe

Child prostitution is a relatively small problem in this region. The two countries that seem to face more problems are Italy and the Netherlands, where 2,000 to 2,500 children are reported victims of child prostitution. The Dutch Institute of Social Sexual Research found that 65 percent of child prostitutes are of Dutch origin or permanent residents. There are two forms of child prostitution in Western Europe: forced prostitution is related to trafficking, and the second type consists mainly of nationals. This population's problem has its root in the lack of adequate support systems for children and of a clear judicial system to deal with the issue.

According to the 1999 report by the U.S. Department of State regarding the sexual exploitation of children in Italy, "[t]here were 1,880 to 2,500 minors working as street prostitutes, of whom 1,500 to 2,300 were trafficked illegal immigrants, predominantly Albanians, and some Nigerians."[13] Another report stated that "[m]ore than 8,000 Albanian prostitutes [are] in Italy, and above 30 percent of them are under 18 years."[14]

Eastern Europe

Child prostitution is a significant problem in this area. Five percent of homeless children in Romania are victims of prostitution. In Russia, it is reported that there are 500,000 street children and that child prostitution makes up approximately 23 percent of the total prostitutes in Moscow. Pimps and gangs control many of these children. Runaway children from dysfunctional homes in Belarus often end up in the railway stations and then are sold to different brothels by pimps. In Eastern Europe, boys are more vulnerable than girls. In Estonia, 881 cases of child sex tourism were reported between 1997 and 1999. In April 2000, two studies found that 80 percent of children aged fourteen to eighteen involved in the study had been paid for sex in the past three months. In Latvia's border regions, children under the age of sixteen are in high demand.

Pacific

A study by ECPAT Australia found approximately 3,000 children in the sex industry in Australia. Child prostitution is on the increase due to the level of poverty resulting from inadequate housing and youth services and increases in homelessness. Sarah Hudson reported that, "more than 3,100 Australian children aged 12-18 sold sex to survive."[15] Reflecting on the seriousness of this issue, Paul Robinson suggested that the seriousness of the problem of pedophilia in Australia has only recently been acknowledged. Sixty percent of the messages posted by The Blue Room Internet bulletin board have to do with child pornography. Of the 450 subscribers, 100 live in Australia.[16] Another report identified

> 5,000 pedophiles who sexually abuse minors and traffic in child pornography operating in loose networks across Australia. They are linked to international pedophile groups including the Spartacus Club, the Marlin Coasters and the Orchid Club. 30,000 girls and 11,000 boys are sexually abused in Australia each year.[17]

Fiji has seen an increase in the number of street children and children entering prostitution. Street children are being picked up and taken to hotels for sex. Girls hang around nightclubs waiting to be picked up. During the Christmas season, a number of children provide sexual services in order to earn money to buy Christmas gifts, while young boys do it to buy toys. In Papua New Guinea, drugs, alcohol, nightlife, and materialism are luring children into the commercial sex industry.

Notes

Introduction

1. One of the men I interviewed is dying of AIDS, and he has also infected his wife.

Chapter 1

1. When I came back from the trip I contacted a number of individuals to see if I could find Ju a sponsor. About a month later, I found one church worker who was willing to help. I tried to contact Ju but learned that she had left the village, leaving no trace of where she had gone. In 1996, I received a letter from a villager who knew Ju. He informed me that Ju was working at Phitsanulok as a servant. I contacted Ju and asked if she would like to go to school. She was thrilled and came right back to her village. She then learned that she could not go to school because she did not have a birth certificate. In a note to me she asked, "Could you send my sister instead?" My response was, "Of course." I told her that I still would like to see her in school and that we could work on getting her a birth certificate. She replied, "That's very generous of you, but can you send my younger brother instead? I think I'm old enough to help support the family. I will go to Bangkok and work in a factory." I was touched by her compassion and sponsored both her brother and her sister to an academy in Chiang Mai. Right now, Yupin, Ju's sister, is completing grade nine and will be attending a vocational school in Chiang Mai. Ju is married and is still sending money to support her family.

2. Cameron W. Barr, "Asia's Traffickers Keep Girls in Sexual Servitude," *The Christian Science Monitor*, p.11. This article first appeared in *The Christian Science Monitor* on August 22, 1996 and is reproduced with permission. © 1996 *The Christian Science Monitor* <www.csmonitor.com>. All rights reserved.

3. Patpong Road is the main red-light district in Bangkok.

4. Montri Sinvichai, *Mur Dek Klai Pen Hyur* (Bangkok: Foundation to Protection Children, 1993), pp. 30-33. According to the report, Nuan escaped the control of her sister and father. She found a job in a restaurant in Bangkok. Due to her psychiatric problem, however, she was again hospitalized in the same hospital. Both her father and sister came to visit. The main content of their visit was "please go back and work in this go-go bar again." The doctor who heard Nuan's story intervened before she was discharged. He contacted the Foundation to Protect Children. Nuan is now staying in this rehabilitation facility in Bangkok.

5. Pasuk Phongpaichit, Sungsidh Piriyarangsan, and Nualnoi Treerat, *Guns, Girls, Gambling, Ganja: Thailand's Illegal Economy and Public Policy* (Chiang Mai: Silkworm Books, 1998), pp. 197-198. See also Wathinee Boonchalaksi and

Philip Guest, *Prostitution in Thailand* (Nakhon Phanom: Institute for Population and Social Research, Mahidol University, 1994), pp. 29-38.

6. Phongpaichit et al., *Guns, Girls, Gambling, Ganja,* p. 200.

7. Wathinee Boonchalaksi and Philip Guest, *Prostitution in Thailand* (Bangkok: Institute for Population and Social Research, Mahidol University, 1994), pp. 29-33.

8. Jenny Godley, "Prostitution in Thailand," in *NIC: Freezone of Prostitution* (Bangkok: Institute for Population and Social Research, Mahidol University, 1991), p. 148.

9. Veerasit Sittirai and Tim Brown, *Female Commercial Sex Workers in Thailand: A Preliminary Report* (Bangkok: Thai Royal Red Cross, 1991).

10. Phongpaichit et al., *Guns, Girls, Gambling, Ganja,* p. 200.

11. Siroj Sorajjakool, "Theological and Psychological Reflection on the Functions of Pastoral Care in the Context of Child Prostitution in Thailand," *Journal of Pastoral Care,* 54 (Winter 2001), p. 430.

12. Aurasom Suthisakorn, *Sanim Dokmai* (Bangkok: Sarakadee Press, 1996), p. 97.

13. Sorajjakool, "Theological and Psychological Reflection," p. 431.

14. Suthisakorn, *Sanim Dokmai,* p. 100.

15. Siroj Sorajjakool, "Child Prostitution: Epidemic & Ethics," *Update,* 16 (2001), pp. 3-4. Other symptoms that commonly appear among teenagers who have been sexually abused are loss of self-esteem and extreme preoccupation with body image. They may become more and more isolated and turn to substance abuse. Others may become sexually precocious. Kathleen Coulborn Faller, *Child Sexual Abuse: An Interdisciplinary Manual for Diagnosis, Case Management, and Treatment* (New York: Columbia University Press, 1988), p. 248.

16. Kahlil Gibran, *Spirit Brides,* trans. Juan R. I. Cole (New York: Penguin, 1998), p. 38.

17. Christopher Baker, "Prostitution: Child Chattel Lure Tourists for Sex," *International,* 21 (1995), p. 10.

Chapter 2

1. Centre for the Protection of Children's Rights, *Annual Report for the Year 1998-99* (Bangkok: CPCR, 1999).

2. Pasuk Phongpaichit, Sungsidh Piriyarangsan, and Nualnoi Treerat, *Guns, Girls, Gambling, Ganja: Thailand's Illegal Economy and Public Policy* (Chiang Mai: Silkworm Books, 1998), p. 167.

3. Cited by Simon Baker, *The Changing Situation of Child Prostitution in Northern Thailand: A Study of Changwat Chiang Rai* (Bangkok: ECPAT International, 2000), p. 32.

4. Wanchai Roujanavong, *Trafficking in Women and Children* (Bangkok: Amarin, 1999), p. 25.

5. Ministry of Labour and Social Welfare, Prevention and Suppression of Prostitution Act, B. E. 2539 (1996), *Government Gazette,* 113 (Part 54 a) (October 22, 1996), p. 5.

6. Ibid., p. 6.

7. Ibid., p. 7.

8. *Salaya dong* means: a shop that sells local liquors.

9. Thai Women of Tomorrow, *Padjai Sahed Hang Kahn Kai Borikarn Tahng Ped Khong Dek Nai Muang Chiang Mai* (Chiang Mai, Thailand: Thai Women of Tomorrow, 1999), p. 25.

Chapter 3

1. Sutin Wannabovorn, "Thailand: Thailand Investigating Why Boy Was Taken to US," *Reuters News Service,* Bangkok (May 4, 2000). Reprinted with permission, copyright Reuters 2002.

2. Hanna Rosin, "Thai Boy Caught Up in Fight Against Sex Trafficking," *Washington Post* (May 15, 2000), p. A02.

3. Paiwarin Khao-Ngam, *Banana Tree Horse*, trans. Birabhongse Kasemsri (Bangkok: Amarin, 1995), p. 9.

4. Ibid., p. 42.

5. Dominique Lapierre, *The City of Joy* (New York: Warner Books, 1985), p. 8.

6. Kanoksak Kaewthep, *Wipark Tun Niyom Thai* (Bangkok: Chulalongkorn Book Center, 1999), p. 14.

7. Siroj Sorajjakool, "Theological and Psychological Reflection on the Functions of Pastoral Care in the Context of Child Prostitution in Thailand," *Journal of Pastoral Care*, 54 (Winter 2001), p. 431.

8. Chattip Narksupa and Pornpilai Lertwicha, *Watanatum Muban Thai* (Bangkok: Sarngsan Publishing, 1994), p. 37.

9. Kaewthep, *Wipark Tun Niyom Thai,* pp. 17-22.

10. Ibid.

11. Nantiya Tangwisutjit, "Poor in Rural Areas to Face Bailout Brunt," *The Nation,* (August 23, 1997), Section: Local. See also, Kaewthep, *Wipark Tun Niyom Thai,* p. 15.

12. Narksupa and Lertwicha, *Watanatum Muban Thai,* p. 35.

13. Ibid., p. 229.

14. Lapierre, *The City of Joy,* p. 8.

15. Khao-Ngam, *Banana Tree Horse,* p. 42.

Chapter 4

1. *Yai* is a pronoun often used to address an elderly woman. It can also be translated as "grandmother."

2. *Kru* is literally translated as "teacher."

3. Padjai Sahed Hang Kahn Kai Borikarn Tahng Ped Khong Dek Nai Muang Chiang Mai (Chiang Mai, Thailand: Thai Women of Tomorrow, 1999), pp. 76-77.

4. Thai Yai is one of the minority groups in northern Thailand.

5. Nitaya Rawangpal and Saovapa Pornsiripong, *AIDS Kub Krabuankarn Kar Pu Ying* (Bangkok: Institute for Linguistic and Cultural Research for Development, Mahidol University, 1996), pp. 88-93.

6. Padjai Sahed Hang Kahn Kai Borikarn Tahng Ped, pp. 14-18.

7. Ibid.

8. Paiwarin Khao-Ngam, *Banana Tree Horse,* trans. Birabhongse Kasemsri (Bangkok: Amarin, 1995), p. 47.

Chapter 5

1. Jeremy Seabrook, *No Hiding Place: Child Sex Tourism and the Role of Extraterritorial Legislation* (New York: Zed Books, 2000), p. xi.
2. Surasak Tumcharoen, "Chalerm Sought Over Sex Claim: Senator Accused of Romp with Minor," *Bangkok Post* (January 22, 2001), p. 1. Reprinted by permission of the *Bangkok Post.*
3. Chalerm Promlert denied the accusation. His lawyer told reporters that he was framed.
4. *Kao Sod* (January 22, 2001), pp. 1, 11.
5. Ron O'Grady, *The Rape of the Innocent: One Million Children Trapped in the Slavery of Prostitution* (Auckland: ECPAT International, 1994), pp. 33-43.
6. Seabrook, *No Hiding Place,* p. 64.
7. O'Grady, *The Rape of the Innocent,* p. 42.
8. "Thai Men Practice Polygamy, Study Says," *Bangkok Post* (February 5, 2001), p. 1.
9. Kathleen C. Faller, *Child Sexual Abuse: An Interdisciplinary Manual for Diagnosis, Case Management, and Treatment* (New York: Columbia University Press, 1988), p. 51.
10. Ibid., p. 56.
11. According to Faller's findings, most psychotic sexual abusers are schizophrenic. Only one of the men in her sample was manic-depressive.
12. Faller, *Child Sexual Abuse,* p. 77.
13. Ibid., p. 79.
14. Ibid., p. 86.
15. Ibid., p. 91.
16. Ibid., p. 41.

Chapter 6

1. Siriporn Sakorbanek, Nuttaya Boonpakdee, and Chutima Chantiro, *Garn Ka Ying: Lur Wi Tee Sangkom Thai* (Bangkok: Women's Foundation, 1997), p. 188.
2. Public Health Department, *Sathanakarn AIDS Nai Chang Wat Chiang Rai* (Chiang Rai Province: Public Health Department, 2000).
3. Chris Lyttleton, *Endangered Relations: Negotiating Sex and AIDS in Thailand* (Bangkok: White Lotus, 2000), p. 104.
4. Public Health Department, *Sathanakarn AID Nai Um Pur Wieng Pa Pao* (Wieng Pa Pao District: Public Health Department, 2000).
5. Lyttleton, *Endangered Relations,* p. 102.
6. AIDS Network Development Project, *Dream Diary* (Ubon Ratchatani: AIDSNet, 1999). Reprinted by permission of the publisher.
7. Ibid., Introduction.
8. Kahlil Gibran, *Spirit Brides,* trans. Juan R. I. Cole (New York: Penguin, 1998), p. 25.

9. AID Network Development Project, *Dream Diary.*

10. Ibid.

11. Paiwarin Khao-Ngam, *Banana Tree Horse,* trans. Birabhongse Kasemsri (Bangkok: Amarin, 1995) p. 87.

Chapter 7

1. Hanna Rosin, "Thai Boy Caught Up in Fight Against Sex Trafficking," *Washington Post* (May 15, 2000), p. A02.

2. According to federal law, INS is given seventy-two hours to locate the child's parents or guardians willing to take care of the minor. If unable to locate parents or guardians, the minor is sent to INS's juvenile facilities, which are run by a nonprofit organization that will try to place the child in foster care. Denise Hamilton, "This Boy's Life," *Los Angeles New Times,* 5(27) (July 6-12, 2000), p. 18.

3. "Mother Joked About Selling Her Son," *Bangkok Post* (May 5, 2000), p. 1.

4. Hamilton, "This Boy's Life," p. 19.

5. Rosin, "Thai Boy Caught Up in Fight," p. A02.

6. Hamilton, "This Boy's Life," p. 19.

7. "Mother Joked About Selling Her Son," p. 1.

8. Ibid.

9. Frans Mulschlegel, "Thai Toddler in US Was Human Smugglers' Prop," *The Nation* (May 10, 2000).

10. Aurasom Suthisakorn, *Sanim Dok Mai* (Bangkok: Sarakadee Press, 1996), p. 107.

11. Hamilton, "This Boy's Life," p. 19. The United Nations also reports that approximately 4 million people are being traded against their will annually. Erin McCormick and Jim Herron Zamora, "Slave Trade Still Alive in U.S.," *San Francisco Examiner* (February 13, 2000).

12. Marjan Wijers and Lin Lap-Chew, *Trafficking in Women, Forced Labour and Slavery-Like Practices in Marriage, Domestic Labour and Prostitution,* Preliminary Report for the Special Rapporteur on Violence Against Women of the UN Human Rights Commission (October, 1996), p. 28.

13. Pasuk Phongpaichit, Sungsidh Piriyarangsan, and Nualnoi Treerat, *Guns, Girls, Gambling, Ganja: Thailand's Illegal Economy and Public Policy* (Chiang Mai: Silkworm Books, 1998), p. 161.

14. Ibid., p. 157.

15. Wanchai Roujanavong, *Trafficking in Women and Children* (Bangkok: Amarin).

16. Ibid.

17. Ibid.

18. Phongpaichit et al., *Guns, Girls, Gambling, Ganja,* p. 155.

19. Ibid., pp. 164-166.

20. Ibid., p. 166.

21. Ibid., pp. 167-171.

22. Wanchai Roujanavong, *Trafficking in Women and Children.*

23. Phongpaichit et al., *Guns, Girls, Gambling, Ganja,* pp. 171-172.

24. Siriporn Sakorbanek, Nuttaya Boonpakdee, and Chutima Chantiro, *Garn Ka Ying: Lur Wi Tee Sangkom Thai* (Bangkok: Foundation for Women, 1997), p. 118.

25. McCormick and Zamora, "Slave Trade Still Alive in U.S.," p. A1. Reprinted by permission of the *San Francisco Examiner.*

26. Ibid.

27. Carey Goldberg, "From Thai Grocery Store to New York Brothel," *Bangkok Post* (September 12, 1995), p. 6.

28. Phongpaichit et al., *Guns, Girls, Gambling, Ganja,* p. 173-174.

29. Kathryn McMahon, "Introduction to the Trafficking of Women: A Report from Los Angeles," unpublished paper, Los Angeles, Coalition to Abolish Slavery and Trafficking, 1999, p. 1. Reprinted by permission of Kathryn McMahon.

30. Kritaya Archavanitkul and Pornsuk Kerdsawang, *The Routes of Women Labourers from Neighbouring Countries into Commercial Sex Businesses in Thailand* (Bangkok: Institute for Population and Social Research, Mahidol University, 1997), pp. 6, 9, 10.

31. Ron O'Grady, *The Rape of the Innocent: One Million Children Trapped in the Slavery of Prostitution* (Auckland: ECPAT International, 1994), p. 16.

32. Kim Gooi, "Hell Hole in Myanmar Brothels," *New Straits Times* (September 2, 1993), p. 1.

33. *The Rape of the Innocent,* pp. 11-22.

34. Phongpaichit et al., *Guns, Girls, Gambling, Ganja,* p. 179.

35. Ibid., p. 179.

36. The name Yunnan comes from the province's location south of Win-ling Mountain. Yunnan comprises 390,000 square kilometers and 40 million people. Its population consists of a large number of ethnic minority groups. Vorasakdi Mahatdhanobol, *Chinese Women in the Thai Sex Trade,* trans. Aaron Stern (Bangkok: Chinese Studies Center, Asian Research Center for Migration, Institute of Asian Studies, Chulalongkorn University, 1998), p. 18.

37. Ibid., pp. 78-80.

38. Ibid., p. 29.

39. Ibid., p. 29.

40. Ibid., p. 41.

41. Simon Baker, *The Changing Situation of Child Prostitution in Northern Thailand: A Study of Changwat Chiang Rai* (Bangkok: ECPAT International, 2000), pp. 33-34.

42. Paiwarin Khao-Ngam, *Banana Tree Horse,* trans. Birabhongse Kasemsri (Bangkok: Amarin, 1995), p. 46.

43. Ibid., p. 47.

Chapter 8

1. *Tanha* is a Buddhist term that means "desire," which is the cause of all suffering. Without desire there would be no suffering, and desire arises out of ignorance.

2. J. Krishnamurti, *In the Light of Silence, All Problems Are Dissolved* (Chennai: Krisnamurti Foundation India, 1992), p. 4.

Afterword

1. ECPAT International, *Looking Back, Thinking Forward: A Fourth Report on the Implementation of the Agenda for Action Adopted at the First World Congress Against Commercial Sexual Exploitation of Children in Stockholm, Sweden, 28 August 1996* (Bangkok: ECPAT International, 2000), p. 108.

Appendix

1. Kathlyn Gay, *Child Labor: A Global Crisis,* (Brookfield, Conn: Millbrook, 1998) citing Joan J. Johnson, *Teen Prostitution* (New York: F. Watts, 1992).

2. "Child Prostitution," *Daily Observer* (October 21, 1996).

3. "Experts Meet in Brazil to Fight Child Sex Slavery," *Bangkok Post* (April 18, 1996).

4. U.S. Department of State, 1999 Country Reports on Human Rights Practices <http://www.state.gov/www/global/human_rights/1999_hrp_report>.

5. Tabibul Islam, "Rape of Minors Worry Parents," *Inter-Press Services,* (April 8, 1998).

6. Brother Jarlath de Souza, "Trafficking in Children: Bangladesh," *Child Workers in Asia* ((12)3 July-September 1996).

7. "Vietnam Child Sex Trade Rising," *Associated Press* (April 24, 1998), citing World Human Rights Organization and UNICEF.

8. Madeline Eisner, "Former Child Prostitute Gets a Chance to Dream Again," *UNICEF Feature,* October 1996.

9. Mikel Flamm and Ngo Kim Cuc, "The Street of Little Flowers," *Bangkok Post* (February 23, 1997).

10. Aphaluck Bhatiasevi, "Influx of Burmese Sex Workers," *Bangkok Post* (June 2, 1997).

11. "Report Cites Burma's Child Rights Abuses," *The Nation* (January 17, 1998).

12. Jacqueline Danam, "Sex Tourism and the Travel Industry," *Travel Trade, Gazette Asia* (October 25-31, 1996), pp. 25-31.

13. U.S. Department of State, 1999 Country Reports on Human Rights Practices <http://www.state.gov/www/global/human_rights/1999_hrp_report>.

14. G.J. Koja, "8000 Albanian Girls Work as Prostitutes in Italy," *HURINet,* (July 25, 1998).

15. Sarah Hudson, "Child Sex Soaring," *Herald Sun* (September 30, 1998).

16. Paul Robinson, "Internet Use by Abusers Ring, Say Investigators," *The Age,* (September 14, 1997).

17. Paul Robinson, "Internet Use by Abusers Ring."

Index

Page numbers followed by the letter "f" indicate figures; those followed by the letter "t" indicate tables.